PUBLISHER COMMENTARY

The Federal Information Technology Acquisition Reform Act (FITARA) made sweeping changes to the ways the U.S. federal government buys and manages computer technology. It became law as a part of the National Defense Authorization Act for Fiscal Year 2015 (Title VIII, Subtitle D, H.R. 3979.

- **Sec. 831** requires specified federal agencies to ensure that the Chief Information Officer (CIO) of the agencies has specified authorities and responsibilities in planning, programming, budgeting, and executing processes related to information technology.
- **Sec. 832** requires the Office of Management and Budget (OMB) to make the cost, schedule, and performance data of specified information technology investments publicly available. Requires the CIO of each agency to categorize the investments according to risk and review those that have a high level of risk.
- **Sec. 833** requires OMB to implement a process to assist specified agencies in reviewing their portfolio of information technology investments, including the development of standardized cost savings and cost avoidance metrics and performance indicators. Requires the CIO of each agency to conduct an annual review of the information technology portfolio and requires the Administrator of the Office of Electronic Government to submit a quarterly report to Congress identifying cost savings and reductions in duplicative investments identified by the review.
- **Sec. 834** provides for the consolidation of federal data centers.
- **Sec. 835** requires OMB to work with federal agencies to update their acquisition human capital plans to address how the agencies are meeting their human capital requirements to support the timely and effective acquisition of information technology.
- **Sec. 836** directs OMB to prescribe regulations requiring a comparative value analysis to be included in the contract file when the federal government purchases services and supplies offered under the Federal Strategic Sourcing Initiative from sources outside the Initiative.
- **Sec. 837** requires the General Services Administration to develop a strategic sourcing initiative to enhance government-wide acquisitions, shared use, and dissemination of software, as well as compliance with end use license agreements.

This book contains the text of the law as enacted, a FITARA Roadmap - Milestone View, the November 2017 Biannual FITARA Scorecard, a June 2015 Memo from the White House that provides implementation guidance, and a GAO statement titled "Further Implementation of FITARA Related Recommendations Is Needed to Better Manage Acquisitions and Operations."

Why buy a book you can download for free? We print this book so you don't have to.
First you gotta find it and you gotta print it using a network printer you share with 100 other people (typically its either out of paper or toner). If it's just a 10-page document, no problem, but if it's 100-pages, you will need to punch 3 holes in all those pages and put it in a 3-ring binder. Takes at least an hour. It's much more cost-effective to just order the latest version from   www.Amazon.com

This material is published by 4th Watch Publishing Co. We publish tightly-bound, full-size books at 8 ½ by 11 inches, with large text and glossy covers. 4th Watch Publishing Co. is a Service Disabled Veteran Owned Small Business (SDVOSB). Please visit www.usgovpub.com.

Other books available on www.Amazon.com :

GAO Green Book - Standards for Internal Control in the Federal Government
GAO Yellow Book - Government Auditing Standards
GAO Financial Audit Manual
DoD 7000.14 - R Financial Management Regulation
Defense Acquisition Guidebook (Chapters 1 - 10)
Federal Acquisition Regulation - Complete
Defense Federal Acquisition Regulation – Complete
OMB No. A-123 - Management's Responsibility for Enterprise Risk Management and Internal Control
OMB A-130 & Federal Information Security Modernization Act (FISMA)
Federal Information System Controls Audit Manual (FISCAM)
GAO Technology Readiness Assessment Guide
GAO Cost Estimating and Assessment Guide
GAO Schedule Assessment Guide

Subtitle D—Federal Information Technology Acquisition Reform

SEC. 831. CHIEF INFORMATION OFFICER AUTHORITY ENHANCEMENTS.

(a) IN GENERAL.—Subchapter II of chapter 113 of title 40, United States Code, is amended by adding at the end the following new section:

10 USC 11319.

"§ 11319. Resources, planning, and portfolio management

"(a) DEFINITIONS.—In this section:

"(1) The term 'covered agency' means each agency listed in section 901(b)(1) or 901(b)(2) of title 31.

"(2) The term 'information technology' has the meaning given that term under capital planning guidance issued by the Office of Management and Budget.

"(b) ADDITIONAL AUTHORITIES FOR CHIEF INFORMATION OFFICERS.—

"(1) PLANNING, PROGRAMMING, BUDGETING, AND EXECUTION AUTHORITIES FOR CIOS.—

"(A) IN GENERAL.—The head of each covered agency other than the Department of Defense shall ensure that the Chief Information Officer of the agency has a significant role in—

"(i) the decision processes for all annual and multi-year planning, programming, budgeting, and execution decisions, related reporting requirements, and reports related to information technology; and

"(ii) the management, governance, and oversight processes related to information technology.

"(B) BUDGET FORMULATION.—The Director of the Office of Management and Budget shall require in the annual information technology capital planning guidance of the Office of Management and Budget the following:

"(i) That the Chief Information Officer of each covered agency other than the Department of Defense approve the information technology budget request of the covered agency, and that the Chief Information Officer of the Department of Defense review and provide recommendations to the Secretary of Defense on the information technology budget request of the Department.

"(ii) That the Chief Information Officer of each covered agency certify that information technology investments are adequately implementing incremental development, as defined in capital planning guidance issued by the Office of Management and Budget.

"(C) REVIEW.—

"(i) IN GENERAL.—A covered agency other than the Department of Defense—

"(I) may not enter into a contract or other agreement for information technology or information technology services, unless the contract or other agreement has been reviewed and approved by the Chief Information Officer of the agency;

"(II) may not request the reprogramming of any funds made available for information technology programs, unless the request has been reviewed and approved by the Chief Information Officer of the agency; and

"(III) may use the governance processes of the agency to approve such a contract or other agreement if the Chief Information Officer of the agency is included as a full participant in the governance processes.

"(ii) DELEGATION.—

"(I) IN GENERAL.—Except as provided in subclause (II), the duties of a Chief Information Officer under clause (i) are not delegable.

"(II) Non-major information technology investments.—For a contract or agreement for a non-major information technology investment, as defined in the annual information technology capital planning guidance of the Office of Management and Budget, the Chief Information Officer of a covered agency other than the Department of Defense may delegate the approval of the contract or agreement under clause (i) to an individual who reports directly to the Chief Information Officer.

"(2) Personnel-related authority.—Notwithstanding any other provision of law, for each covered agency other than the Department of Defense, the Chief Information Officer of the covered agency shall approve the appointment of any other employee with the title of Chief Information Officer, or who functions in the capacity of a Chief Information Officer, for any component organization within the covered agency.

"(c) Limitation.—None of the authorities provided in this section shall apply to telecommunications or information technology that is fully funded by amounts made available—

"(1) under the National Intelligence Program, defined by section 3(6) of the National Security Act of 1947 (50 U.S.C. 3003(6));

"(2) under the Military Intelligence Program or any successor program or programs; or

"(3) jointly under the National Intelligence Program and the Military Intelligence Program (or any successor program or programs).".

(b) Clerical Amendment.—The table of sections for chapter 113 of title 40, United States Code, is amended by inserting after the item relating to section 11318 the following new item:

10 USC prec. 11301.

"11319. Resources, planning, and portfolio management.".

SEC. 832. ENHANCED TRANSPARENCY AND IMPROVED RISK MANAGEMENT IN INFORMATION TECHNOLOGY INVESTMENTS.

Section 11302(c) of title 40, United States Code, is amended—

(1) by redesignating paragraphs (1) and (2) as paragraphs (2) and (5), respectively;

(2) by inserting before paragraph (2), as so redesignated, the following new paragraph (1):

"(1) Definitions.—In this subsection:

"(A) The term 'covered agency' means an agency listed in section 901(b)(1) or 901(b)(2) of title 31.

"(B) The term 'major information technology investment' means an investment within a covered agency information technology investment portfolio that is designated by the covered agency as major, in accordance with capital planning guidance issued by the Director.

"(C) The term 'national security system' has the meaning provided in section 3542 of title 44."; and

(3) by inserting after paragraph (2), as so redesignated, the following new paragraphs:

"(3) Public availability.—

"(A) In general.—The Director shall make available to the public a list of each major information technology investment, without regard to whether the investments are for new information technology acquisitions or for operations and maintenance of existing information technology, including data on cost, schedule, and performance.

"(B) AGENCY INFORMATION.—

"(i) The Director shall issue guidance to each covered agency for reporting of data required by subparagraph (A) that provides a standardized data template that can be incorporated into existing, required data reporting formats and processes. Such guidance shall integrate the reporting process into current budget reporting that each covered agency provides to the Office of Management and Budget, to minimize additional workload. Such guidance shall also clearly specify that the investment evaluation required under subparagraph (C) adequately reflect the investment's cost and schedule performance and employ incremental development approaches in appropriate cases.

"(ii) The Chief Information Officer of each covered agency shall provide the Director with the information described in subparagraph (A) on at least a semi annual basis for each major information technology investment, using existing data systems and processes.

"(C) INVESTMENT EVALUATION.—For each major information technology investment listed under subparagraph (A), the Chief Information Officer of the covered agency, in consultation with other appropriate agency officials, shall categorize the investment according to risk, in accordance with guidance issued by the Director.

"(D) CONTINUOUS IMPROVEMENT.—If either the Director or the Chief Information Officer of a covered agency determines that the information made available from the agency's existing data systems and processes as required by subparagraph (B) is not timely and reliable, the Chief Information Officer, in consultation with the Director and the head of the agency, shall establish a program for the improvement of such data systems and processes.

"(E) WAIVER OR LIMITATION AUTHORITY.—The applicability of subparagraph (A) may be waived or the extent of the information may be limited by the Director, if the Director determines that such a waiver or limitation is in the national security interests of the United States.

"(F) ADDITIONAL LIMITATION.—The requirements of subparagraph (A) shall not apply to national security systems or to telecommunications or information technology that is fully funded by amounts made available—

"(i) under the National Intelligence Program, defined by section 3(6) of the National Security Act of 1947 (50 U.S.C. 3003(6));

"(ii) under the Military Intelligence Program or any successor program or programs; or

"(iii) jointly under the National Intelligence Program and the Military Intelligence Program (or any successor program or programs).

"(4) RISK MANAGEMENT.—For each major information technology investment listed under paragraph (3)(A) that receives a high risk rating, as described in paragraph (3)(C), for 4 consecutive quarters—

"(A) the Chief Information Officer of the covered agency and the program manager of the investment within the covered agency, in consultation with the Administrator of the Office of Electronic Government, shall conduct a review of the investment that shall identify—

"(i) the root causes of the high level of risk of the investment;

"(ii) the extent to which these causes can be addressed; and

"(iii) the probability of future success;

"(B) the Administrator of the Office of Electronic Government shall communicate the results of the review under subparagraph (A) to—

"(i) the Committee on Homeland Security and Governmental Affairs and the Committee on Appropriations of the Senate;

"(ii) the Committee on Oversight and Government Reform and the Committee on Appropriations of the House of Representatives; and

"(iii) the committees of the Senate and the House of Representatives with primary jurisdiction over the agency;

"(C) in the case of a major information technology investment of the Department of Defense, the assessment required by subparagraph (A) may be accomplished in accordance with section 2445c of title 10, provided that the results of the review are provided to the Administrator of the Office of Electronic Government upon request and to the committees identified in subsection (B); and

"(D) for a covered agency other than the Department of Defense, if on the date that is one year after the date of completion of the review required under subsection (A), the investment is rated as high risk under paragraph (3)(C), the Director shall deny any request for additional development, modernization, or enhancement funding for the investment until the date on which the Chief Information Officer of the covered agency determines that the root causes of the high level of risk of the investment have been addressed, and there is sufficient capability to deliver the remaining planned increments within the planned cost and schedule.

"(5) SUNSET OF CERTAIN PROVISIONS.—Paragraphs (1), (3), and (4) shall not be in effect on and after the date that is 5 years after the date of the enactment of the Carl Levin and Howard P. 'Buck' McKeon National Defense Authorization Act for Fiscal Year 2015.".

SEC. 833. PORTFOLIO REVIEW.

Section 11319 of title 40, United States Code, as added by section 831, is amended by adding at the end the following new section:

"(c) INFORMATION TECHNOLOGY PORTFOLIO, PROGRAM, AND RESOURCE REVIEWS.—

"(1) PROCESS.—The Director of the Office of Management and Budget, in consultation with the Chief Information Officers of appropriate agencies, shall implement a process to assist covered agencies in reviewing their portfolio of information technology investments—

"(A) to identify or develop ways to increase the efficiency and effectiveness of the information technology investments of the covered agency;

"(B) to identify or develop opportunities to consolidate the acquisition and management of information technology services, and increase the use of shared-service delivery models;

"(C) to identify potential duplication and waste;

"(D) to identify potential cost savings;

"(E) to develop plans for actions to optimize the information technology portfolio, programs, and resources of the covered agency;

"(F) to develop ways to better align the information technology portfolio, programs, and financial resources of the covered agency to any multi-year funding requirements or strategic plans required by law;

"(G) to develop a multi-year strategy to identify and reduce duplication and waste within the information technology portfolio of the covered agency, including component-level investments and to identify projected cost savings resulting from such strategy; and

"(H) to carry out any other goals that the Director may establish.

"(2) METRICS AND PERFORMANCE INDICATORS.—The Director of the Office of Management and Budget, in consultation with the Chief Information Officers of appropriate agencies, shall develop standardized cost savings and cost avoidance metrics and performance indicators for use by agencies for the process implemented under paragraph (1).

"(3) ANNUAL REVIEW.—The Chief Information Officer of each covered agency, in conjunction with the Chief Operating Officer or Deputy Secretary (or equivalent) of the covered agency and the Administrator of the Office of Electronic Government, shall conduct an annual review of the information technology portfolio of the covered agency.

"(4) APPLICABILITY TO THE DEPARTMENT OF DEFENSE.—In the case of the Department of Defense, processes established pursuant to this subsection shall apply only to the business systems information technology portfolio of the Department of Defense and not to national security systems as defined by section 11103(a) of this title. The annual review required by paragraph (3) shall be carried out by the Deputy Chief Management Officer of the Department of Defense (or any successor to such Officer), in consultation with the Chief Information Officer, the Under Secretary of Defense for Acquisition, Technology, and Logistics, and other appropriate Department of Defense officials. The Secretary of Defense may designate an existing investment or management review process to fulfill the requirement for the annual review required by paragraph (3), in consultation with the Administrator of the Office of Electronic Government.

"(5) QUARTERLY REPORTS.—

"(A) IN GENERAL.—The Administrator of the Office of Electronic Government shall submit a quarterly report on the cost savings and reductions in duplicative information technology investments identified through the review required by paragraph (3) to—

"(i) the Committee on Homeland Security and Governmental Affairs and the Committee on Appropriations of the Senate;

"(ii) the Committee on Oversight and Government Reform and the Committee on Appropriations of the House of Representatives; and

"(iii) upon a request by any committee of Congress, to that committee.

"(B) INCLUSION IN OTHER REPORTS.—The reports required under subparagraph (A) may be included as part of another report submitted to the committees of Congress described in clauses (i), (ii), and (iii) of subparagraph (A).

"(6) SUNSET.—This subsection shall not be in effect on and after the date that is 5 years after the date of the enactment of the Carl Levin and Howard P. 'Buck' McKeon National Defense Authorization Act for Fiscal Year 2015.".

44 USC 3601 note.

SEC. 834. FEDERAL DATA CENTER CONSOLIDATION INITIATIVE.

(a) DEFINITIONS.—In this section:

(1) ADMINISTRATOR.—The term "Administrator" means the Administrator of the Office of Electronic Government established under section 3602 of title 44, United States Code (and also known as the Office of E-Government and Information Technology), within the Office of Management and Budget.

(2) COVERED AGENCY.—The term "covered agency" means the following (including all associated components of the agency):

(A) Department of Agriculture.
(B) Department of Commerce.
(C) Department of Defense.
(D) Department of Education.
(E) Department of Energy.
(F) Department of Health and Human Services.
(G) Department of Homeland Security.
(H) Department of Housing and Urban Development.
(I) Department of the Interior.
(J) Department of Justice.
(K) Department of Labor.
(L) Department of State.
(M) Department of Transportation.
(N) Department of Treasury.
(O) Department of Veterans Affairs.
(P) Environmental Protection Agency.
(Q) General Services Administration.
(R) National Aeronautics and Space Administration.
(S) National Science Foundation.
(T) Nuclear Regulatory Commission.
(U) Office of Personnel Management.
(V) Small Business Administration.
(W) Social Security Administration.
(X) United States Agency for International Development.

(3) FDCCI.—The term "FDCCI" means the Federal Data Center Consolidation Initiative described in the Office of Management and Budget Memorandum on the Federal Data

Center Consolidation Initiative, dated February 26, 2010, or any successor thereto.

(4) GOVERNMENT-WIDE DATA CENTER CONSOLIDATION AND OPTIMIZATION METRICS.—The term "Government-wide data center consolidation and optimization metrics" means the metrics established by the Administrator under subsection (b)(2)(G).

(b) FEDERAL DATA CENTER CONSOLIDATION INVENTORIES AND STRATEGIES.—

(1) IN GENERAL.—

(A) ANNUAL REPORTING.—Except as provided in subparagraph (C), each year, beginning in the first fiscal year after the date of the enactment of this Act and each fiscal year thereafter, the head of each covered agency, assisted by the Chief Information Officer of the agency, shall submit to the Administrator—

(i) a comprehensive inventory of the data centers owned, operated, or maintained by or on behalf of the agency; and

(ii) a multi-year strategy to achieve the consolidation and optimization of the data centers inventoried under clause (i), that includes—

(I) performance metrics—

(aa) that are consistent with the Government-wide data center consolidation and optimization metrics; and

(bb) by which the quantitative and qualitative progress of the agency toward the goals of the FDCCI can be measured;

(II) a timeline for agency activities to be completed under the FDCCI, with an emphasis on benchmarks the agency can achieve by specific dates;

(III) year-by-year calculations of investment and cost savings for the period beginning on the date of the enactment of this Act and ending on the date set forth in subsection (e), broken down by each year, including a description of any initial costs for data center consolidation and optimization and life cycle cost savings and other improvements, with an emphasis on—

(aa) meeting the Government-wide data center consolidation and optimization metrics; and

(bb) demonstrating the amount of agency-specific cost savings each fiscal year achieved through the FDCCI; and

(IV) any additional information required by the Administrator.

(B) USE OF OTHER REPORTING STRUCTURES.—The Administrator may require a covered agency to include the information required to be submitted under this subsection through reporting structures determined by the Administrator to be appropriate.

(C) DEPARTMENT OF DEFENSE REPORTING.—For any year that the Department of Defense is required to submit a performance plan for reduction of resources required for data servers and centers, as required under section 2867(b) of the National Defense Authorization Act for Fiscal Year 2012 (10 U.S.C. 2223a note), the Department of Defense—

(i) may submit to the Administrator, in lieu of the multi-year strategy required under subparagraph (A)(ii)—

(I) the defense-wide plan required under section 2867(b)(2) of the National Defense Authorization Act for Fiscal Year 2012 (10 U.S.C. 2223a note); and

(II) the report on cost savings required under section 2867(d) of the National Defense Authorization Act for Fiscal Year 2012 (10 U.S.C. 2223a note); and

(ii) shall submit the comprehensive inventory required under subparagraph (A)(i), unless the defense-wide plan required under section 2867(b)(2) of the National Defense Authorization Act for Fiscal Year 2012 (10 U.S.C. 2223a note)—

(I) contains a comparable comprehensive inventory; and

(II) is submitted under clause (i).

(D) STATEMENT.—Each year, beginning in the first fiscal year after the date of the enactment of this Act and each fiscal year thereafter, the head of each covered agency, acting through the Chief Information Officer of the agency, shall—

(i)(I) submit a statement to the Administrator stating whether the agency has complied with the requirements of this section; and

(II) make the statement submitted under subclause (I) publicly available; and

(ii) if the agency has not complied with the requirements of this section, submit a statement to the Administrator explaining the reasons for not complying with such requirements.

(E) AGENCY IMPLEMENTATION OF STRATEGIES.—

(i) IN GENERAL.—Each covered agency, under the direction of the Chief Information Officer of the agency, shall—

(I) implement the strategy required under subparagraph (A)(ii); and

(II) provide updates to the Administrator, on a quarterly basis, of—

(aa) the completion of activities by the agency under the FDCCI;

(bb) any progress of the agency towards meeting the Government-wide data center consolidation and optimization metrics; and

(cc) the actual cost savings and other improvements realized through the implementation of the strategy of the agency.

(ii) DEPARTMENT OF DEFENSE.—For purposes of clause (i)(I), implementation of the defense-wide plan required under section 2867(b)(2) of the National Defense Authorization Act for Fiscal Year 2012 (10

U.S.C. 2223a note) by the Department of Defense shall be considered implementation of the strategy required under subparagraph (A)(ii).

(F) RULE OF CONSTRUCTION.—Nothing in this section shall be construed to limit the reporting of information by a covered agency to the Administrator, the Director of the Office of Management and Budget, or Congress.

(2) ADMINISTRATOR RESPONSIBILITIES.—The Administrator shall—

(A) establish the deadline, on an annual basis, for covered agencies to submit information under this section;

(B) establish a list of requirements that the covered agencies must meet to be considered in compliance with paragraph (1);

(C) ensure that information relating to agency progress towards meeting the Government-wide data center consolidation and optimization metrics is made available in a timely manner to the general public;

(D) review the inventories and strategies submitted under paragraph (1) to determine whether they are comprehensive and complete;

(E) monitor the implementation of the data center strategy of each covered agency that is required under paragraph (1)(A)(ii);

(F) update, on an annual basis, the cumulative cost savings realized through the implementation of the FDCCI; and

(G) establish metrics applicable to the consolidation and optimization of data centers Government-wide, including metrics with respect to—

(i) costs;

(ii) efficiencies, including, at a minimum, server efficiency; and

(iii) any other factors the Administrator considers appropriate.

(3) COST SAVING GOAL AND UPDATES FOR CONGRESS.—

(A) IN GENERAL.—Not later than one year after the date of the enactment of this Act, the Administrator shall develop, and make publicly available, a goal, broken down by year, for the amount of planned cost savings and optimization improvements achieved through the FDCCI during the period beginning on the date of the enactment of this Act and ending on the date set forth in subsection (e).

(B) ANNUAL UPDATE.—

(i) IN GENERAL.—Not later than one year after the date on which the goal described in subparagraph (A) is made publicly available, and each year thereafter, the Administrator shall aggregate the reported cost savings of each covered agency and optimization improvements achieved to date through the FDCCI and compare the savings to the projected cost savings and optimization improvements developed under subparagraph (A).

(ii) UPDATE FOR CONGRESS.—The goal required to be developed under subparagraph (A) shall be submitted to Congress and shall be accompanied by a statement describing—

(I) the extent to which each covered agency has developed and submitted a comprehensive inventory under paragraph (1)(A)(i), including an analysis of the inventory that details specific numbers, use, and efficiency level of data centers in each inventory; and

(II) the extent to which each covered agency has submitted a comprehensive strategy that addresses the items listed in paragraph (1)(A)(ii).

(4) GAO REVIEW.—

(A) IN GENERAL.—Not later than one year after the date of the enactment of this Act, and each year thereafter, the Comptroller General of the United States shall review and verify the quality and completeness of the inventory and strategy of each covered agency required under paragraph (1)(A).

(B) REPORT.—The Comptroller General of the United States shall, on an annual basis, publish a report on each review conducted under subparagraph (A).

(c) ENSURING CYBERSECURITY STANDARDS FOR DATA CENTER CONSOLIDATION AND CLOUD COMPUTING.—

(1) IN GENERAL.—In implementing a data center consolidation and optimization strategy under this section, a covered agency shall do so in a manner that is consistent with Federal guidelines on cloud computing security, including—

(A) applicable provisions found within the Federal Risk and Authorization Management Program (FedRAMP); and

(B) guidance published by the National Institute of Standards and Technology.

(2) RULE OF CONSTRUCTION.—Nothing in this section shall be construed to limit the ability of the Director of the Office of Management and Budget to update or modify the Federal guidelines on cloud computing security.

(d) WAIVER OF REQUIREMENTS.—The Director of National Intelligence and the Secretary of Defense, or their respective designee, may waive the applicability to any national security system, as defined in section 3542 of title 44, United States Code, of any provision of this section if the Director of National Intelligence or the Secretary of Defense, or their respective designee, determines that such waiver is in the interest of national security. Not later than 30 days after making a waiver under this subsection, the Director of National Intelligence or the Secretary of Defense, or their respective designee, shall submit to the Committee on Homeland Security and Governmental Affairs and the Select Committee on Intelligence of the Senate and the Committee on Oversight and Government Reform and the Permanent Select Committee on Intelligence of the House of Representatives a statement describing the waiver and the reasons for the waiver.

(e) SUNSET.—This section is repealed effective on October 1, 2018.

41 USC 1704
note.

SEC. 835. EXPANSION OF TRAINING AND USE OF INFORMATION TECH-NOLOGY CADRES.

(a) PURPOSE.—The purpose of this section is to ensure timely progress by Federal agencies toward developing, strengthening, and deploying information technology acquisition cadres consisting of personnel with highly specialized skills in information technology acquisition, including program and project managers.

(b) STRATEGIC PLANNING.—

(1) IN GENERAL.—The Administrator for Federal Procurement Policy, in consultation with the Administrator for E-Government and Information Technology, shall work with Federal agencies, other than the Department of Defense, to update their acquisition human capital plans that were developed pursuant to the October 27, 2009, guidance issued by the Administrator for Federal Procurement Policy in furtherance of section 1704(g) of title 41, United States Code (originally enacted as section 869 of the Duncan Hunter National Defense Authorization Act for Fiscal Year 2009 (Public Law 110–417; 122 Stat. 4553)), to address how the agencies are meeting their human capital requirements to support the timely and effective acquisition of information technology.

(2) ELEMENTS.—The updates required by paragraph (1) shall be submitted to the Administrator for Federal Procurement Policy and shall address, at a minimum, each Federal agency's consideration or use of the following procedures:

(A) Development of an information technology acquisition cadre within the agency or use of memoranda of understanding with other agencies that have such cadres or personnel with experience relevant to the agency's information technology acquisition needs.

(B) Development of personnel assigned to information technology acquisitions, including cross-functional training of acquisition information technology and program personnel.

(C) Use of the specialized career path for information technology program managers as designated by the Office of Personnel Management and plans for strengthening information technology program management.

(D) Use of direct hire authority.

(E) Conduct of peer reviews.

(F) Piloting of innovative approaches to information technology acquisition workforce development, such as industry-government rotations.

(c) FEDERAL AGENCY DEFINED.—In this section, the term "Federal agency" means each agency listed in section 901(b) of title 31, United States Code.

41 USC 3301
note.

SEC. 836. MAXIMIZING THE BENEFIT OF THE FEDERAL STRATEGIC SOURCING INITIATIVE.

Not later than 180 days after the date of the enactment of this Act, the Administrator for Federal Procurement Policy shall prescribe regulations providing that when the Federal Government makes a purchase of services and supplies offered under the Federal Strategic Sourcing Initiative (managed by the Office of Federal Procurement Policy) but such Initiative is not used, the contract file for the purchase shall include a brief analysis of the comparative value, including price and nonprice factors, between the services and supplies offered under such Initiative and services and supplies offered under the source or sources used for the purchase.

10 USC 3301 note.

SEC. 837. GOVERNMENTWIDE SOFTWARE PURCHASING PROGRAM.

(a) IN GENERAL.—The Administrator of General Services shall identify and develop a strategic sourcing initiative to enhance Governmentwide acquisition, shared use, and dissemination of software, as well as compliance with end user license agreements.

(b) GOVERNMENTWIDE USER LICENSE AGREEMENT.—The Administrator, in developing the initiative under subsection (a), shall allow for the purchase of a license agreement that is available for use by all Executive agencies (as defined in section 105 of title 5, United States Code) as one user to the maximum extent practicable and as appropriate.

FITARA Roadmap - Milestone View

As of: March 20, 2018

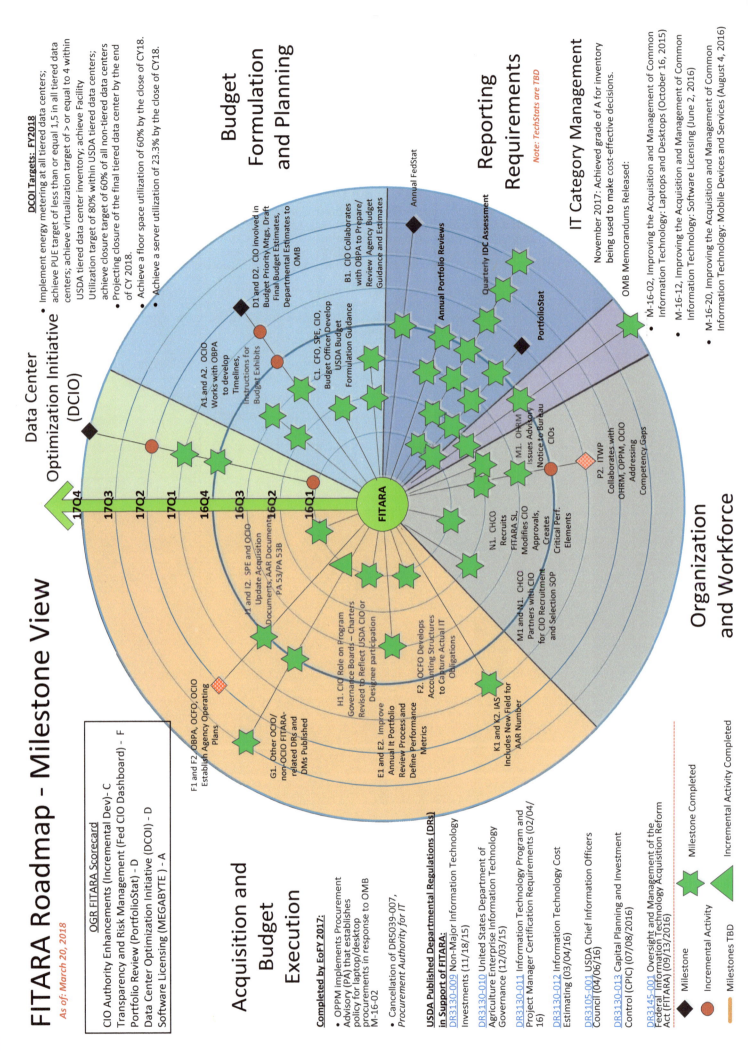

OGR FITARA Scorecard

CIO Authority Enhancements (Incremental Dev)- C
Transparency and Risk Management (Fed CIO Dashboard) - F
Portfolio Review (PortfolioStat) - D
Data Center Optimization Initiative (DCOI) - D
Software Licensing (MEGABYTE) - A

Acquisition and Budget Execution

Completed by EoFY 2017:

• OPPM implements Procurement Advisory (PA) that establishes policy for laptop/desktop procurements in response to OMB M-16-02

• Cancellation of DR5039-007, *Procurement Authority for IT*

USDA Published Departmental Regulations (DRs) in Support of FITARA:

DR3130-009 Non-Major Information Technology Investments (11/18/15)

DR3130-010 United States Department of Agriculture Enterprise Information Technology Governance (12/03/15)

DR3130-011 Information Technology Program and Project Manager Certification Requirements (02/04/16)

DR3130-012 Information Technology Cost Estimating (03/04/16)

DR3105-001 USDA Chief Information Officers Council (04/06/16)

DR3130-013 Capital Planning and Investment Control (CPIC) (07/08/2016)

DR3145-001 Oversight and Management of the Federal Information Technology Acquisition Reform Act (FITARA) (09/13/2016)

Legend:
★ Milestone Completed
★ Incremental Activity Completed
◆ Milestone
● Incremental Activity
▬ Milestones TBD

DCOI Targets: FY2018
• Implement energy metering at all tiered data centers; achieve PUE target of less than or equal 1.5 in all tiered data centers; achieve virtualization target of > or equal to 4 within USDA tiered data center inventory; achieve Facility Utilization target of 80% within USDA tiered data centers;
• achieve closure target of 60% of all non-tiered data centers by the end of CY 2018.
• Projecting closure of the final tiered data center by the close of CY18.
• Achieve a floor space utilization of 60% by the close of CY18.
• Achieve a server utilization of 23.3% by the close of CY18.

Budget Formulation and Planning

Reporting Requirements
Note: TechStats are TBD

IT Category Management

November 2017: Achieved grade of A for inventory being used to make cost-effective decisions.

OMB Memorandums Released:

• M-16-02, Improving the Acquisition and Management of Common Information Technology: Laptops and Desktops (October 16, 2015)
• M-16-12, Improving the Acquisition and Management of Common Information Technology: Software Licensing (June 2, 2016)
• M-16-20, Improving the Acquisition and Management of Common Information Technology: Mobile Devices and Services (August 4, 2016)

Data Center Optimization Initiative (DCIO)

Organization and Workforce

FITARA

Annual FedStat

Annual Portfolio Reviews

Quarterly IDC Assessment

PortfolioStat

D1 and D2. CIO involved in Budget Priority Mtgs, Draft Final Budget Estimates, Departmental Estimates to OMB

B1. CIO Collaborates with OBPA to Prepare/ Review Agency Budget Guidance and Estimates

A1 and A2. OCIO Works with OBPA to develop Timelines, Instructions for Budget Exhibits

C1. CFO, SPE, CIO, Budget Officer Develop USDA Budget Formulation Guidance

M1. OHRM Issues Advisory Notice to Bureau CIOs

P2. ITWP Collaborates with OHRM, OPPM, OCIO Addressing Competency Gaps

N1. CHCO Recruits FITARA SL, Modifies CIO Approvals, Creates Critical Perf. Elements

M1 and N1. CHCO Partners with CIO for CIO Recruitment and Selection SOP

F1 and F2. OBPA, OCFO, OCIO Establish Agency Operating Plans

G1. Other OCIO/ non-OCIO FITARA-related DRs and DMs Published

I1 and I2. SPE and OCIO Update Acquisition Documents, AAR Document PA 53/PA 53B

H1. CIO Role on Program Governance Boards – Charters Revised to Reflect USDA CIO or Designee participation

E1 and E2. Improve Annual It Portfolio Review Process and Define Performance Metrics

F2. OCFO Develops Accounting Structures to Capture Actual IT Obligations

K1 and K2. IAS Includes New Field for AAR Number

17Q4
17Q3
17Q2
17Q1
16Q4
16Q3
16Q2
16Q1

OGR Biannual FITARA Scorecard

	Nov '15 Grade		May '16 Grade		Dec '16 Grade		Jun '17 Grade		Nov '17 Grade
USDA	D	▲	C	=	C-	=	C-	=	C-
DOC	B	=	B	=	B+	▼	B+	=	B+
DOD	D	=	D	=	D+	▼	F+	=	F+
Ed.	F	▲	D	▲	C+	=	C+	▲	B+
Energy	F	▲	C	=	C-	=	C-	▼	D+
HHS	D	=	D	=	D-	=	D-	=	D-
DHS	C	=	C	▲	B-	=	B-	▼	C-
HUD	D	=	D	▲	C-	▲	B-	▼	C-
DOI	C	=	C	▲	B+	=	C+	=	C+
DOJ	D	▲	C	=	B-	=	B-	▼	C-
DOL	D	▲	C	=	C-	▼	D-	=	D-
State	D	=	D	=	D-	▲	C-	=	C-
DOT	D	=	D	▼	F+	▲	D+	▼	F+
Treas.	D	=	D	▲	C-	=	C-	=	C-
VA	C	=	C	▲	B+	=	B+	=	B+
EPA	C	=	C	▲	B+	=	B+	▼	C+
GSA	B	▼	C	▲	B+	=	B+	=	B+
NASA	F	=	F	▲	C+	=	C+	=	C+
NSF	D	=	D	▲	C-	=	C-	=	C-
NRC	C	=	C	=	C-	=	C-	=	C-
OPM	D	▲	C	=	C+	=	D+	▲	C+
SBA	D	=	D	=	D-	=	D-	=	D-
SSA	D	▲	C	▲	B+	▼	C+	=	C+
USAID	D	=	D	=	D+	▲	A+	=	A-

Changes				
▲ 7	▲ 12	▲ 4	▲ 3	
= 16	= 11	= 15	= 15	
▼ 1	▼ 1	▼ 5	▼ 6	

	Agency CIO authority enhancements — Incremental	Transparency and risk management — Dashboard	Portfolio review — PortfolioStat	Data center optimization Initiative — DCOI	Software Licensing — MEGABYTE	CIO's boss = Sec/Dep Sec	CIO Status
USDA	C	F	D	D	A	N	Acting
DOC	B	A	A	C	F	Y	Acting
DOD	F	C	F	F	F	Y	Acting
Ed.	A	D	D	A	A	Y	Permanent
Energy	A	D	D	F	F	Y	Permanent
HHS	A	B	F	F	F	N	Permanent
DHS	B	C	B	C	F	N	Permanent
HUD	A	A	F	A	F	N	Permanent
DOI	A	D	B	F	F	Y	Permanent
DOJ	A	C	B	B	F	N	Permanent
DOL	D	B	D	F	C	N	Permanent
State	A	A	C	C	F	N	Permanent
DOT	F	F	C	F	F	Y	Permanent
Treas.	D	C	A	B	F	N	Acting
VA	A	B	B	F	A	Y	Permanent
EPA	A	A	C	C	F	Y	Acting
GSA	A	C	B	A	A	Y	Permanent
NASA	F	F	A	B	A	Y	Permanent
NSF	A	F	C	B	F	N	Acting
NRC	A	D	D	C	F	N	Permanent
OPM	A	B	F	D	F	Y	Permanent
SBA	A	D	C	C	F	N	Permanent
SSA	D	B	A	C	F	Y	Permanent
USAID	A	A	A	B	A	N	Permanent
	All software proj.	Tiers / DOD alt source	Tiers / JSONS	50-50 Bumps	Include		

Grade distribution (left):

Grade	Nov '15		May '16		Dec '16		Jun '17		Nov '17
A							▲ 1	=	1
B	2	▼	1	▲	8		7		4
C	5	▲	12	▼	10	=	10	▲	14
D	14	▼	10	▼	5	=	5	▼	3
F	3	▼	1	=	1	=	1	▲	2

Category distribution (right):

Grade	Incremental	Dashboard	PortfolioStat	DCOI	MEGABYTE
A	15	5	5	3	6
B	2	5	5	5	
C	1	5	5	7	1
D	3	5	5	2	
F	3	4	4	7	17

12 Y	18 permanent
12 N	6 acting

June 10, 2015

THE DIRECTOR

M-15-14

MEMORANDUM FOR HEADS OF EXECUTIVE DEPARTMENTS AND AGENCIES

FROM: Shaun Donovan
             Director

SUBJECT: Management and Oversight of Federal Information Technology

Purpose

The purpose of this memorandum is to provide implementation guidance for the Federal Information Technology Acquisition Reform Act (FITARA)[1] and related information technology (IT) management practices.

Background

FITARA was enacted on December 19, 2014. FITARA outlines specific requirements related to:

1. Agency Chief Information Officer (CIO) Authority Enhancements
2. Enhanced Transparency and Improved Risk Management in IT Investments
3. Portfolio Review
4. Federal Data Center Consolidation Initiative
5. Expansion of Training and Use of IT Cadres
6. Maximizing the Benefit of the Federal Strategic Sourcing Initiative
7. Governmentwide Software Purchasing Program

To implement the requirements of FITARA, combined with the need to update policy and guidance related to other modern IT practices, OMB is publishing this guidance. This guidance reflects input from a diverse group of stakeholders, including representatives from the Chief Financial Officer (CFO), Chief Human Capital Officer (CHCO), Chief Acquisition Officer (CAO), Assistant Secretary for Management (ASAM), Chief Operating Officer (COO), and CIO communities.

Objectives

The objectives of the requirements outlined in this memorandum are to:

1. Assist agencies in establishing management practices that align IT resources with agency missions, goals, programmatic priorities, and statutory requirements;
2. Establish governmentwide IT management controls that will meet FITARA requirements while providing agencies with the flexibility to adapt to agency processes and unique mission requirements;

---

[1] Title VIII, Subtitle D of the National Defense Authorization Act (NDAA) for Fiscal Year 2015, Pub. L. No. 113-291. Further references in the text that refer to "FITARA" refer to these sections.

3. Establish a "Common Baseline" for roles, responsibilities, and authorities of the agency CIO and the roles and responsibilities of other applicable Senior Agency Officials[2] in managing IT as a strategic resource;

4. Enable the CIO's role, with respect to the development, integration, delivery, and operations of any type of IT, IT service, or information product to enable integration with the capabilities they support wherever IT may affect functions, missions, or operations;

5. Strengthen the agency CIO's accountability for the agency's IT cost, schedule, performance, and security;

6. Strengthen the relationship between agency CIOs and bureau CIOs;

7. Establish consistent governmentwide interpretation of FITARA terms and requirements;

8. Assist agencies in establishing an inclusive governance process that will enable effective planning, programming, budgeting, and execution for IT resources;

9. Provide transparency on IT resources across entire agencies and programs; and

10. Provide appropriate visibility and involvement of the agency CIO in the management and oversight of IT resources across the agency to support the successful implementation of cybersecurity policies to prevent interruption or exploitation of program services.

Scope and Applicability

1. Covered agencies: CFO Act agencies[3] and their divisions and offices are subject to the requirements outlined in FITARA and this memorandum, except where otherwise noted. The Department of Defense (DOD), the Intelligence Community, and portions of other agencies that operate systems related to national security are subject to only certain portions of FITARA, as provided for in the statute, and shall meet with OMB no later than 60 days following the final release of this guidance to clarify the applicability of this guidance throughout their organizations and activities, including alternative requirements or exceptions.

2. Additionally, all other Executive Branch agencies are encouraged to apply the principles described in this guidance to their management of IT, consistent with their legal authorities.

3. Covered agencies shall implement this guidance in a manner consistent with other legal authorities and should consult with their counsel regarding those authorities.

4. With respect to Offices of Inspectors General (OIG), this guidance should be implemented in a manner that does not impact the independence of those offices and the authorities Inspectors General have over the personnel, performance, procurement, and budget of the OIG, as provided in the Inspector General Act of 1978, as amended (5 U.S.C. App 3).

5. This memorandum builds upon and will refer to existing OMB policy and guidance.

6. Where possible, this guidance incorporates agency reporting requirements introduced by FITARA into existing OMB processes, such as PortfolioStat, the Integrated Data Collection (IDC),[4] Acquisition Human Capital Planning, and the Federal IT Dashboard (ITDB), rather than creating new reporting channels and tools.

7. With respect to Federal statistical agencies and units as defined in the Confidential Information Protection and Statistical Efficiency Act of 2002 (CIPSEA),[5] covered agencies under FITARA shall implement this guidance in a manner that ensures that statistical data collected under a pledge of confidentiality solely for statistical purposes are used exclusively for statistical purposes, consistent with CIPSEA.

---

[2] Senior Agency Officials, as referred to in this guidance, include positions such as the CFO, CHCO, CAO, ASAM, COO, and Program Manager.
[3] Agencies listed in 31 U.S.C. § 901 (b)(1) and (b)(2).
[4] M-14-08 FY2014 PortfolioStat Guidance available at: https://www.whitehouse.gov/sites/default/files/omb/memoranda/2014/m-14-08.pdf.
[5] 44 U.S.C. § 3501 note

Table of Contents

This document is organized into a main body and a series of attachments.

Section A: Defining the Scope of Resources Related to Information Technology

Many of the requirements of this memorandum refer to the agency CIO's involvement with the decision processes and policies related to "information technology resources" throughout the agency, including IT within programs. To establish a consistent governmentwide interpretation of the Federal resources included in this scope, the following definition shall be used for "information technology resources:"

1. "Information technology resources" includes all:

    A. Agency budgetary resources, personnel, equipment, facilities, or services that are primarily used in the management, operation, acquisition, disposition, and transformation, or other activity related to the lifecycle of information technology;

    B. Acquisitions or interagency agreements that include information technology and the services or equipment provided by such acquisitions or interagency agreements; but

    C. Does not include grants to third parties which establish or support information technology not operated directly by the Federal Government.

2. This definition and this memorandum refer to the term "information technology," which for the purposes of this memorandum is defined as:

    A. Any services or equipment, or interconnected system(s) or subsystem(s) of equipment, that are used in the automatic acquisition, storage, analysis, evaluation, manipulation, management, movement, control, display, switching, interchange, transmission, or reception of data or information by the agency; where

    B. such services or equipment are 'used by an agency' if used by the agency directly or if used by a contractor under a contract with the agency that requires either use of the services or equipment or requires use of the services or equipment to a significant extent in the performance of a service or the furnishing of a product.

C. The term "information technology" includes computers, ancillary equipment (including imaging peripherals, input, output, and storage devices necessary for security and surveillance), peripheral equipment designed to be controlled by the central processing unit of a computer, software, firmware and similar procedures, services (including provisioned services such as cloud computing and support services that support any point of the lifecycle of the equipment or service), and related resources.

D. The term "information technology" does not include any equipment that is acquired by a contractor incidental to a contract that does not require use of the equipment.

This definition is based on the definition of information technology found in the Clinger-Cohen Act of 1996.[6] Additional definitions used in this memorandum are available in *Attachment A*.

Revising other IT management policies to reflect this scope

To establish consistency across IT management and acquisition policies, OMB Circular A-130, OMB Circular A-11, and the Federal Acquisition Regulation (FAR) will be updated to reflect these definitions of "information technology resources" and "information technology," as appropriate.

Section B: Implementation of the Common Baseline

1. The "Common Baseline" (*Attachment A*) provides guidance on the CIO's and other Senior Agency Officials' roles and responsibilities for the management of IT. This Common Baseline provides a framework for agencies to implement the specific authorities that FITARA provides for CFO Act agency CIOs, and builds upon their responsibilities as outlined in the Clinger-Cohen Act of 1996.[7] The Common Baseline also speaks to the roles and responsibilities of other Senior Agency Officials, as it is critical that these officials in each covered agency are engaged in the oversight of IT investments.

2. All covered agencies shall institute policies and procedures that implement the roles, responsibilities, and requirements found in the Common Baseline. The Common Baseline provides agencies with certain flexibility to adopt procedures that meet these requirements in a manner tailored to the volume and type of work completed by the agencies. As explained further in *Attachment A*, agencies may adopt a plan that provides for the CIO's direct involvement or a framework approved by the CIO that contains clear rules on the procedures by which decisions are made and articulates that the CIO remains responsible and accountable for those decisions (referred to as the "CIO Assignment Plan" in *Attachment A*). Further detail is provided in the "CIO Assignment Plan" section found in *Attachment A*.

3. Each agency shall take the following actions to implement the Common Baseline:

   • **Complete agency self-assessment and plan.** Each covered agency shall conduct a self-assessment that identifies current conformity with or gaps in conformity with the Common Baseline, and shall articulate an implementation plan describing the changes it will make to

---

[6] Clinger-Cohen Act (40 U.S.C. §§ 11101-11704) available at http://www.gpo.gov/fdsys/pkg/USCODE-2013-title40/html/USCODE-2013-title40-subtitleIII.htm.
[7] Ibid.

ensure that all Common Baseline responsibilities described in *Attachment A* are implemented by December 31, 2015. This shall include a discussion of how agency senior leaders and program leaders will work in partnership to facilitate the successful implementation of the Common Baseline and how the agency CIO will be enabled as a strategic partner integrated in shaping Agency strategies, budgets, and operations. The deputy secretary or chief operating officer or higher is responsible for the completion of the self-assessment and plan documents. This self-assessment and implementation plan shall not exceed 25 pages and shall include the template in *Attachment C* or another template approved by OMB.

- **Submit to OMB for acceptance of self-assessment and implementation plan.** Covered agencies shall submit this self-assessment and this implementation plan for review and approval to OMB's Office of E-Government & Information Technology (E-Gov) as well as to the agency's relevant OMB Resource Management Office no later than August 15, 2015. To fulfill this requirement, the agency deputy secretary or chief operating officer or higher is responsible for submitting these documents by email to egov@omb.eop.gov with the subject line: "[Agency Abbreviation] FITARA Common Baseline Implementation Plan." OMB may request additional information from agencies before the self-assessment and implementation plan are approved. Agencies shall post the implementation plan portion of this document (posting the self-assessment is optional but encouraged) on their public website at agency.gov/digitalstrategy, and include it as a downloadable dataset in their Public Data Listing,[8] no more than 30 days following OMB approval and thereafter keep the public document up to date with access to a history of previous versions.

- **Support ongoing oversight of implementation plan and Common Baseline.** Covered agencies shall follow OMB guidance from PortfolioStat sessions and other oversight activities regarding the ongoing implementation of the Common Baseline. Agencies shall notify OMB of any obstacles or incomplete implementation of the Common Baseline on an ongoing basis following the initial implementation deadline. OMB may request agencies to revise or update agency self-assessments or implementation plans during implementation as more information becomes available about the agency's management processes.

- **Conduct annual review and update to self-assessment.** Covered agencies shall update the self-assessment annually to identify any obstacles or incomplete implementation of Common Baseline responsibilities that occurred over the preceding 12 months. The first update will be due April 30, 2016, and each April 30 on an annual basis thereafter.

4. The following additional actions will be taken to support agencies' implementation of the Common Baseline:

- **Federal CIO Council (the Council) shall develop and share on-going support and tools.** Through the end of fiscal year (FY) 2016, the Council will dedicate time in its meetings to discuss current topics related to the implementation of the Common Baseline at least once every quarter. The Council should consult with the CFO Council in the development of materials to support changes related to the Common Baseline across management domains. The Council will also assist agencies in implementing the Common Baseline by sharing examples of agency governance processes and IT policies on a public website at https://management.cio.gov.

---

[8] See *Open Data Policy-Managing Information as an Asset* (M-13-13) available at:
https://www.whitehouse.gov/sites/default/files/omb/memoranda/2013/m-13-13.pdf.

- **Support President's Management Council (PMC) follow-up.** By June 30, 2015, the PMC will select three members from the Council to provide an update on governmentwide implementation of FITARA on a quarterly basis through the end of FY2016. These updates will improve each agency's awareness of policies and processes which have worked well at other agencies.

Section C: Transparency, Risk Management, Portfolio Review, and Reporting

1. Covered agencies shall continue to report required data to OMB as part of the quarterly IDC per current instructions. OMB will continue to update IDC instructions posted on the MAX Federal Community on a quarterly basis.[9]

   - **Standardized cost savings metrics and performance indicators.** As a part of the IDC reporting requirements, agencies shall continue to provide cost savings and cost avoidance achieved as a result of strategies that the agency has decided to adopt. Based on this information, agencies will be provided a summary scorecard that provides agency-specific performance metric data and portfolio analysis agenda items.

   - **Sharing with the public and Congress.** As required by the Consolidated and Further Continuing Appropriations Act, 2015 (P.L. 113-235)[10] OMB will continue to report quarterly to Congress on the cost savings, avoidance, and reductions in duplicative IT investments resulting from the above agency efforts. OMB will also provide a summary of these savings by agency on a publicly accessible website. Agency reporting requirements for these topics are included in the IDC instructions.

2. Covered agencies shall continue to provide information to the ITDB, as required by OMB's capital planning and investment control (CPIC) guidance, which is issued annually in conjunction with the release of OMB Circular A-11.[11] As a part of that guidance, the following approaches will be used to meet FITARA requirements:

   - **Monthly reporting.** Covered agencies shall continue to provide updates of risks, performance metrics, project, and activity data for major IT investments to the ITDB as soon as the data becomes available, or at least once each calendar month.

   - **Data improvement program.** If OMB or the agency CIO determines data reported to the ITDB is not timely and reliable, the CIO (in consultation with the agency head) must notify OMB through the IDC and establish within 30 days of this determination an improvement program to address the deficiencies. The CIO will collaborate with OMB to develop a plan that includes root cause analysis, timeline to resolve, and lessons learned. In addition, the CIO will communicate to OMB the steps the agency is taking to execute the data improvement program and the progress the agency is making. Agencies will provide updates on the status of this program on a quarterly basis as a part of their IDC submission until the identified deficiency is resolved.

---

[9] See https://community.max.gov/x/LhtGJw.

[10] Public law 113-235 contains: "Provided further, That the Director of the Office of Management and Budget shall submit quarterly reports not later than 45 days after the end of each quarter to the Committees on Appropriations of the House of Representatives and the Senate and the Government Accountability Office identifying the savings achieved by the Office of Management and Budget's governmentwide information technology reform efforts: Provided further, That such reports shall include savings identified by fiscal year, agency, and appropriation."

[11] OMB Circular A-11 available at: https://www.whitehouse.gov/omb/circulars_a11_current_year_a11_toc. OMB IT budget capital planning guidance available at: https://www.whitehouse.gov/omb/e-gov/strategiesandguides.

- **TechStat Sessions.** A TechStat is a face-to-face, evidence-based accountability review of an IT program with agency leadership.[12] TechStat sessions are a tool for getting ahead of critical problems in an investment, turning around underperforming investments, or terminating investments if appropriate. For all agency-led TechStat reviews of investments, the agency shall contact egov@omb.eop.gov with the subject line, "[Agency Acronym] TechStat Notification," at least two weeks ahead of the TechStat session. Agencies shall follow the agency's TechStat policy and procedures based on the CIO.gov TechStat Toolkit when managing TechStat sessions. Agencies shall report the outcomes and outputs of all TechStat sessions through the quarterly IDC, including: the assessment described in *Attachment E: Investment and Portfolio Management Maturity Framework*, a root cause analysis of performance issues, corrective action plans which address these causes, and a timeline for implementing the corrective actions. More detailed reporting guidance will be provided in the quarterly IDC instructions.

- **High risk rating.** Given the size and complexity of the multi-billion dollar Federal IT Portfolio, it is critical to maintain a focus on the health of IT investments across the government. As required by CPIC guidance, the CIO evaluations reported to the ITDB for all major IT investments must reflect the CIO's assessment of the current level of risk for any major investment's ability to accomplish its goals based on factors described in the CPIC guidance.

- **Automatic TechStats.** Moreover, if an investment has a high risk rating (red CIO evaluation in the ITDB) for three consecutive months beginning July 1, 2015, agencies must hold a TechStat session on that investment. The session must be held within 30 days of the completion of the third month. If this investment remains categorized with a red CIO evaluation one year following the TechStat session then OMB may take appropriate performance and/or budgetary actions until the agency has addressed the root cause and ensured the investment's ability to complete the remaining activities within planned cost and schedule.

3. As explained in Attachment D, PortfolioStat is a data-driven tool that agencies use to assess the current maturity of their IT portfolio management processes and select PortfolioStat action items to strengthen their IT portfolio. Covered agencies shall hold PortfolioStat sessions on a quarterly basis with OMB, the agency CIO, and other attendees. (These sessions were previously annual and required the attendance of the agency deputy secretary (see *Implementing PortfolioStat* (M-12-10)[13], *Fiscal Year 2013 PortfolioStat Guidance: Strengthening Federal IT Portfolio Management* (M-13-09),[14] and *Fiscal Year 2014 PortfolioStat* (M-14-08)).[15]

   During these sessions, agencies will:[16]

   - Discuss and update a multi-year strategy to identify and reduce duplication and waste within the IT portfolio of the agency, including component-level investments and to identify projected cost savings resulting from such strategy;
   - Identify or develop ways to increase the efficiency and effectiveness of the IT investments of the agency;

---

[12] *CIO.gov TechStat Toolkit* available at: https://cio.gov/drivingvalue/techstat/browse-toolkit/.

[13] *Implementing PortfolioStat* (M-12-10) available at: http://www.whitehouse.gov/sites/default/files/omb/memoranda/2012/m-12-10_1.pdf

[14] Fiscal Year 2013 PortfolioStat Guidance: Strengthening Federal IT Portfolio Management (M-13-09) available at: https://www.whitehouse.gov/sites/default/files/omb/memoranda/2013/m-13-09.pdf.

[15] *Fiscal Year 2014 PortfolioStat* (M-14-08) available at: https://www.whitehouse.gov/sites/default/files/omb/memoranda/2014/m-14-08.pdf.

[16] The following bullets reflect requirements outlined in FITARA Section 833 (c)(1).

- Identify or develop opportunities to increase the use of shared-service delivery models;
- Identify potential duplication and waste;
- Develop plans for actions to optimize the IT portfolio, programs, and resources of the agency;
- Review investments included in High Impact Programs; and
- Develop ways to better align the IT portfolio, programs, and financial resources of the agency to long term mission requirements or strategic plans required by law.

Agencies must report the status of PortfolioStat action items in the IDC at least quarterly. Annually by April 30, agency heads shall review and certify the status of PortfolioStat action items with the agency CIO and send to OMB.

OMB will focus on the metrics highlighted in PortfolioStat materials, data submitted through the quarterly IDC process, and agency IT Major Business Case information developed through the CPIC process to assess agency PortfolioStat progress. Complete FY 2015 PortfolioStat guidance is included in *Attachment D*.

Section D: Federal Data Center Consolidation Initiative (FDCCI)

OMB FDCCI Guidance,[17] which was issued in March 2012, outlined the goals, responsibilities, and reporting requirements for agencies through the end of FY 2015. Covered agencies shall continue to provide updates regarding phase one of FDCCI in their quarterly IDC submissions. OMB will publish updated FDCCI guidance by the end of FY 2015, which will describe the second phase of the initiative and will refresh and refocus the data center optimization strategy on the efficient and effective use of resources and implementation of the statutory requirements of FITARA.

---

[17] Implementation Guidance for the Federal Data Center Consolidation Initiative (March 2012) available at
https://www.whitehouse.gov/sites/default/files/omb/assets/egov_docs/cio_memo_fdcci_deliverables_van_roekel_3-19-12.pdf.

Section E: Information Technology Acquisition Initiatives

1. <u>IT Acquisition Cadres</u>. FITARA's requirements for IT acquisition cadres builds upon OMB's Office of Federal Procurement Policy (OFPP) July 2011 memorandum on building specialized IT acquisition cadres.[18] As originally required by the memorandum, *Acquisition Workforce Development Strategic Plan for Civilian Agencies – FY 2010 – 2014*[19] of October 27, 2009, civilian CFO Act agencies shall continue to send their annual *Acquisition Human Capital Plans* to OMB OFPP. The latest iteration of those Plans was due April 15, 2015.

   Additional guidance from OMB issued in February 2015 requires agencies to address new reporting elements required by FITARA. Details regarding these new reporting elements are found in *Attachment F*.

2. <u>Category Management and the Federal Strategic Sourcing Initiative (FSSI)</u>.[20] Agencies will be required to comply with an upcoming new rule regarding purchases of services and supplies of types offered under an FSSI agreement without using an FSSI agreement. In February 2015, the FAR Council initiated rulemaking to implement this provision of FITARA, which creates a preference for strategically sourced vehicles. Once finalized, agencies will be required to include in the contract file a brief analysis of the comparative value, including price and non-price factors, between the services and supplies offered under the FSSI and services and supplies offered under the source or sources used for the purchase. This rule will be in addition to other strategies that OFPP is developing around category management, a practice adopted by industry where spending is managed by categories of common spending, like IT and Transportation, and led by experts who promote governmentwide best practices and help agencies avoid unnecessary duplicative spending and activities. OMB formally launched the Category Management initiative[21] in December 2014.

3. <u>Governmentwide Software Purchasing Program</u>. The General Services Administration (GSA), in collaboration with OMB, shall create, and allow agencies access to, governmentwide enterprise software licenses through new awards as part of category management. These awards shall, at a minimum, allow for the purchase of a license agreement that is available for use by all Executive agencies.[22]

---

[18] *Guidance for Specialized Information Technology Acquisition Cadres*,
https://www.whitehouse.gov/sites/default/files/omb/procurement/memo/guidance-for-specialized-acquisition-cadres.pdf.
[19] *Acquisition Workforce Development Strategic Plan for Civilian Agencies – FY 2010 – 2014*,
http://www.whitehouse.gov/sites/default/files/omb/assets/procurement_workforce/AWF_Plan_10272009.pdf.
[20] *M-13-02, Improving Acquisition through Strategic Sourcing, December 5, 2012*,
https://www.whitehouse.gov/sites/default/files/omb/memoranda/2013/m-13-02_0.pdf.
[21] *OMB Memorandum, Transforming the Marketplace: Simplifying Federal Procurement to Improve Performance, Drive Innovation, and Increase Savings, December 4, 2014*, https://www.whitehouse.gov/sites/default/files/omb/procurement/memo/simplifying-federal-procurement-to-improve-performance-drive-innovation-increase-savings.pdf.
[22] As defined in 5 U.S.C. § 105.

Attachment A: Common Baseline for IT Management and CIO Assignment Plan

All covered agencies shall adopt specific controls for the management of IT from the "Common Baseline" below. The Common Baseline prescribes a basic set of specific responsibilities and processes that all covered agencies shall have in place **no later than December 31, 2015**. A set of definitions follows the Common Baseline to further clarify the specific responsibilities.

Throughout the Common Baseline:

- All references to "CIO" refer to department/headquarters CIOs, and only references to "bureau CIO" refer to the CIO or official-with-CIO-duties within a bureau or any component organization of the agency (see definitions).

- If an agency has a "budget officer" separate from the CFO, then references to "CFO" shall also refer to the budget officer.

- If an agency has a "senior procurement executive" separate from the CAO, then references to "CAO" shall refer also to the senior procurement executive.

DOD, the Intelligence Community, and portions of other agencies that operate systems related to national security are subject to only certain portions of FITARA and shall meet with OMB no later than 60 days following the final release of this guidance to clarify the applicability of this guidance throughout their organizations and activities, including alternative requirements or exceptions.

Common Baseline for IT Management and CIO Assignment Plan

Statutory Language (FITARA unless otherwise noted)	1. CIO Role and Responsibilities	2. CXO/Other Roles and Responsibilities
Budget Formulation and Planning		
The head of each covered agency ... shall ensure that the Chief Information Officer of the agency has a <u>significant role</u> in—"(i) the decision processes for all annual and multi-year <u>planning, programming, budgeting, and execution decisions</u>" *40 U.S.C. § 11319(b)(1)(A)*	A1. **Visibility of IT resource plans/decisions to CIO.** The CFO and CIO jointly shall define the level of detail with which IT resource levels are described distinctly from other resources throughout the planning, programming, and budgeting stages. This should serve as the primary input into the IT capital planning and investment control documents submitted with the budget (formerly Exhibits 53 and 300). B1. **CIO role in pre-budget submission for programs that include IT and overall portfolio.** The agency head shall ensure the agency-wide budget development process includes the CFO, CAO, and CIO in the planning, programming, and budgeting stages for programs that include IT resources (not just programs that are primarily IT oriented). The agency head, in consultation with the CFO, CIO, and program leadership, shall define the processes by that program leadership works with the CIO to plan an overall portfolio of IT resources that achieve program and business objectives and to develop sound estimates of the necessary IT resources for accomplishing those objectives. C1. **CIO role in planning program management.** The CIO shall be included in the internal planning processes for how the agency uses IT resources to achieve its objectives. The CIO shall approve the IT components of any plans, through a process defined by the agency head that balances IT investments with other uses of agency funding. This includes CIO involvement with planning for IT resources at all points in their lifecycle, including operations and disposition or migration.	A2. **Visibility of IT resource plans/decisions in budget materials.** The CFO and CIO jointly shall define the level of detail with which IT resource levels are described as detailed in A1. B2. **CIO role in pre-budget submission for programs that include IT and overall portfolio.** The agency head shall ensure the agency-wide budget development process includes the CFO, CAO, and CIO as described in B1 and that CIO guidelines are applied to the planning of all IT resources during budget formulation. The CFO and program leadership shall work jointly with the CIO to establish the processes and definitions described in B1. C2. **CIO role in program management.** CIO, CFO, and program leadership shall define an agency-wide process by that the CIO shall advise on all planning described in C1.
BUDGET FORMULATION.—The Director of the Office of Management and Budget shall require in the annual information technology capital planning guidance of the Office of Management and Budget the following:"(i) That the Chief Information Officer of each covered agency ... <u>approve the information technology budget request</u> of the covered agency. *40 U.S.C. § 11319 (b)(1)(B)(i)*	D1. **CIO reviews and approves major IT investment portion of budget request.** Agency budget justification materials in their initial budget submission to OMB shall include a statement that affirms: • the CIO has reviewed and approves the major IT investments portion of this budget request; • the CFO and CIO jointly affirm that the CIO had a significant role in reviewing planned IT support for major program objectives and significant increases and decreases in IT resources; and • the IT Portfolio (formerly Exhibit 53) includes appropriate estimates of all IT resources included in the budget request.	D2. **CIO and CFO Certify IT Portfolio.** The CFO shall work with the CIO to establish the affirmations in D1.

Statutory Language (FITARA unless otherwise noted)	1. CIO Role and Responsibilities	2. CXO/Other Roles and Responsibilities
The head of each covered agency … shall ensure that the Chief Information Officer of the agency has a significant role in—(i) the decision processes for all annual and multi-year planning, programming, budgeting, and execution decisions… and (ii) the management, governance and oversight processes related to [IT]… *40 U.S.C. § 11319(b)(1)(A)* The Director of the Office of Management and Budget shall require in the annual information technology capital planning guidance of the Office of Management and Budget the following: That the Chief Information Officer of each covered agency certify that information technology investments are adequately implementing incremental development, as defined in	E1. **Ongoing CIO engagement with program managers.** The CIO should establish and maintain a process to regularly engage with program managers supporting each agency strategic objective. It should be the CIO and program managers' shared responsibility to ensure that legacy and on-going IT investments are appropriately delivering customer value and meeting the business objectives of programs. F1. **Visibility of IT planned expenditure reporting to CIO.** The CFO, CAO and CIO should define agency-wide policy for the level of detail of planned expenditure reporting for all transactions that include IT resources. G1. **CIO defines IT processes and policies.** The CIO defines the development processes, milestones, review gates, and the overall policies for all capital planning, enterprise architecture, and project management and reporting for IT resources. At a minimum, these processes shall ensure that the CIO certifies that IT resources are adequately implementing incremental development (as defined in the below definitions). The CIO should ensure that such processes and policies address each category of IT resources appropriately—for example, it may not be appropriate to apply the same process or policy to highly customized mission-specific applications and back office enterprise IT systems depending on the agency environment. These policies shall be posted publicly at agency.gov/digitalstrategy, included as a downloadable dataset in the agency's Public Data Listing, and shared with OMB through the IDC. For more information, see OMB Circular A-130: Management of Information Resources. H1. **CIO role on program governance boards.** In order to ensure early matching of appropriate IT with program objectives, the CIO shall be a member of governance boards that include IT resources (including "shadow IT" or "hidden IT"—see definitions), including bureau Investment Review Boards (IRB). The CIO shall notify OMB of all governance boards the CIO is a member of and at least annually update this notification.	E2. **Ongoing CIO engagement with program managers.** Program managers shall work with the CIO to define IT performance metrics and strategies to support fulfillment of agency strategic objectives defined in the agency's strategic plan. F2. **Visibility of IT planned expenditure reporting to CIO.** The CFO, CAO and CIO shall define agency-wide policy for the level of detail of planned expenditure reporting for all transactions that include IT resources. H2. Participate with CIO on governance boards as appropriate.

Acquisition and Execution

	Statutory Language (FITARA unless otherwise noted)	1. CIO Role and Responsibilities	2. CXO/Other Roles and Responsibilities
	capital planning guidance issued by the Office of Management and Budget. *40 U.S.C. § 11319*	I1. **Shared acquisition and procurement responsibilities.** The CIO reviews all cost estimates of IT related costs and ensures all acquisition strategies and acquisition plans that include IT apply adequate incremental development principles (see definitions).	I2. **Shared acquisition and procurement responsibilities.** The CAO, in consultation with the CIO and—where appropriate—CFO, shall ensure there is an agency-wide process to ensure all acquisitions that include any IT: • are led by personnel with appropriate federal acquisition certifications (FACs)[23], including specialized IT certifications as appropriate; • are reviewed for opportunities to leverage acquisition initiatives such as shared services, category management, strategic sourcing, and incremental or modular contracting and use such approaches as appropriate; • are supported by cost estimates that have been reviewed by the CIO; and • adequately implement incremental development.
	The CIO… monitors the performance of information technology programs of the agency, evaluates the performance of those programs on the basis of the applicable performance measurements, and advises the head of the agency regarding whether to continue, modify, or terminate a program or project; *40 USC §11315(c)(2)*	J1. **CIO role in recommending modification, termination, or pause of IT projects or initiatives.** The CIO shall conduct TechStat reviews or use other applicable performance measurements to evaluate the use of the IT resources of the agency. The CIO may recommend to the agency head the modification, pause, or termination of any acquisition, investment, or activity that includes a significant IT component based on the CIO's evaluation, within the terms of the relevant contracts and applicable regulations.	
	IN GENERAL.—A covered agency other than the Department of Defense— (I) may not enter into a contract or other agreement for information technology or information technology services, unless the contract or other agreement has been reviewed and approved by the Chief Information Officer of the agency; *40 U.S.C. § 11319 (b)(1)(C)(i)(I)*	K1. **CIO review and approval of acquisition strategy and acquisition plan.** Agencies shall not approve an acquisition strategy or acquisition plan (as described in FAR Part 7[24]) or interagency agreement (such as those used to support purchases through another agency) that includes IT without review and approval by the agency CIO. For contract actions that contain IT without an approved acquisition strategy or acquisition plan, the CIO shall review and approve the action itself. The CIO shall primarily consider the following factors when reviewing acquisition strategies and acquisition plans: • Appropriateness of contract type; • Appropriateness of IT related portions of statement of needs or statement of work; • Appropriateness of above with respect to the mission and business objectives supported by the IT strategic plan; and • Alignment with mission and program objectives in consultation with program leadership.	K2. **CAO is responsible for ensuring contract actions that contain IT are consistent with CIO-approved acquisition strategies and plans.** The CAO shall indicate to the CIO when planned acquisition strategies and acquisition plans include IT. The CAO shall ensure the agency shall initiate no contract actions or interagency agreements that include IT unless they are reviewed and approved by the CIO or are consistent with the acquisition strategy and acquisition plan previously approved by the CIO. **Similar process for contract modifications.** CAO shall also ensure that no modifications that make substantial changes to the scope of a significant contract are approved that are inconsistent with the acquisition strategy and acquisition plan previously approved by the CIO unless the modification is reviewed and approved by the CIO.

[23] Federal acquisition certifications such as FAC-C (Contracting), FAC-P/PM (Project and Program Managers), and FAC-COR (Contracting Officers Representative).
[24] Federal Acquisition Regulation: Part 7 available at http://www.acquisition.gov/far/html/FARTOCP07.html.

Statutory Language (FITARA unless otherwise noted)	1. CIO Role and Responsibilities	2. CXO/Other Roles and Responsibilities
IN GENERAL.—A covered agency…— "(II) may not request the reprogramming of any funds made available for information technology programs, unless the request has been reviewed and approved by the Chief Information Officer of the agency *40 U.S.C. § 11319 (b)(1)(C)(i)(II)*	**L1. CIO approval of reprogramming.** The CIO must approve any movement of funds for IT resources that requires Congressional notification.	**L2. CIO approval of reprogramming.** The CFO shall ensure any notifications under L1 are approved by the CIO prior to submission to OMB.
PERSONNEL-RELATED AUTHORITY.— Notwithstanding any other provision of law, for each covered agency … the Chief Information Officer of the covered agency shall approve the appointment of any other employee with the title of Chief Information Officer, or who functions in the capacity of a Chief Information Officer, for any component organization within the covered agency. *40 U.S.C. 11319 (b)(2)* Delegation of authority… (b) In addition to the authority to delegate conferred by other law, the head of an agency may delegate to subordinate officials the authority vested in him–(1) by law to take final action on matters pertaining to the employment, direction, and general administration of personnel under his agency… *5 U.S.C. 302 (b)(1)*	**M1. CIO approves bureau CIOs.** The CIO shall be involved in the recruitment and shall approve the selection of any new bureau CIO (includes bureau leadership with CIO duties but not title—see definitions). The title and responsibilities of current bureau CIOs may be designated or transferred to other agency personnel by the agency head or his or her designee as appropriate, and such decisions may take into consideration recommendations from the agency CIO.	
The Chief Information Officer of an agency… (A) assesses the requirements established for agency personnel regarding knowledge and skill in information resources management and the adequacy of those requirements for facilitating the achievement of the	**N1. CIO role in ongoing bureau CIOs' evaluations.** The CHCO and CIO shall jointly establish an agency-wide critical element (or elements) included in all bureau CIOs' performance evaluations. In cases where the bureau CIO is a member of the Senior Executive Service and the agency uses the Basic SES Appraisal System, this critical element(s) is an "agency-specific performance requirement" in the Executive Performance Plan. Each such agency may determine that critical element(s) (ECQs) contain these requirements. For agencies that do not use the Basic SES Appraisal System or for bureau CIOs who are not members of the SES, then these shall be critical elements in their evaluations. The [agency] CIO must identify "key bureau CIOs" and provide input to the rating official for this critical element(s) for at least all "key bureau CIOs" at the time of the initial summary rating and for any required progress reviews. The rating official will consider the input from the [agency] CIO when determining the initial summary rating and discusses it with the bureau CIO during progress reviews.	**N2. CIO role in ongoing bureau CIOs' evaluations.** The CHCO and CIO shall jointly establish an agency-wide critical element (or elements) for the evaluation of bureau CIOs as described in N1.

Organization and Workforce

Statutory Language (FITARA unless otherwise noted)	1. CIO Role and Responsibilities	2. CXO/Other Roles and Responsibilities
performance goals established for information resources management; (B) assesses the extent to which the positions and personnel at the executive level of the agency and the positions and personnel at management level of the agency below the executive level meet those requirements; 40 U.S.C. § 11315(c)(3) (Clinger-Cohen Act)	O1. **Bureau IT Leadership Directory.** CIO and CHCO will conduct a survey of all bureau CIOs and CHCO will jointly publish a dataset identifying all bureau officials with title of CIO or duties of a CIO. This shall be posted as a public dataset based on instructions in the IDC by August 15, 2015 and kept up- to- date thereafter. The report will identify for each: • Employment type (e.g. GS, SES, SL, ST, etc.) • Type of appointment (e.g. career, appointed, etc.) • Other responsibilities (e.g. full-time CIO or combination CIO/CFO) • Evaluation "rating official" (e.g. bureau head, other official) • Evaluation "reviewing official" (if used) • Whether [agency] CIO identifies this bureau CIO as a "key bureau CIO" and thus requires the [agency] CIO to provide the rating official input into the agency-wide critical element(s) described in N1. P1. **IT Workforce.** The CIO and CHCO will develop a set of competency requirements for IT staff, including IT leadership positions, and develop and maintain a current workforce planning process to ensure the department/agency can (a) anticipate and respond to changing mission requirements, (b) maintain workforce skills in a rapidly developing IT environment, and (c) recruit and retain the IT talent needed to accomplish the mission.	O2. **Bureau IT Leadership Directory.** CHCO will work with CIO to develop the Bureau IT Leadership Directory as described in O1. P2. **IT Workforce.** CIO and CHCO—and CAO where relevant—shall develop a set of competency requirements for IT staff, including IT leadership positions, and develop and maintain a current workforce planning process to ensure the department/agency can (a) anticipate and respond to changing mission requirements, (b) maintain IT workforce skills in a rapidly developing IT environment, and (c) recruit and retain the IT talent needed to accomplish the mission.
The head of each agency shall designate a Chief Information Officer who shall report directly to such agency head to carry out the responsibilities of the agency under this subchapter. 44 U.S.C. § 3506 (Clinger-Cohen Act)	Q1. **CIO reports to agency head (or deputy/COO).** As required by the Clinger Cohen Act and left in place by FITARA, the CIO "shall report directly to such agency head to carry out the responsibilities of the agency under this subchapter." This provision remains unchanged, though certain agencies have since implemented legislation under which the CIO and other management officials report to a COO, Undersecretary for Management, Assistant Secretary for Administration, or similar management executive; in these cases, to remain consistent with the Clinger Cohen requirement as left unchanged by FITARA, the CIO shall have direct access to the agency head (i.e., the Secretary, or Deputy Secretary serving on the Secretary's behalf) regarding programs that include information technology.	

Common Baseline for IT Management and CIO Assignment Plan

(continued)

CIO Assignment Plan

It is critical that the agency CIO retain accountability for the roles and responsibilities identified in the Common Baseline. As agency environments vary considerably, CIOs may find that decisions about some IT resources included in the Common Baseline may be more appropriately executed by other agency officials, such as a bureau CIO or even parts of program or procurement communities. This must be done in a way to allow the agency CIO to retain accountability.

For the responsibilities other than those detailed in D1 and M1 of the above chart (budget approval and bureau CIO appointment), the CIO may designate other agency officials to act as a representative of the CIO in aspects of the above processes in a rules-based manner, such as by a dollar threshold, type of planned IT activity, or by bureau. This designation shall be developed in consultation with the CFO, CAO, CHCO, and other Senior Agency Officials, as appropriate. Even if a representative is substituted for the CIO, the CIO retains accountability for the assigned role or responsibility and thus must ensure the overall suitability of selected officials. Because the selected official represents the CIO, CIOs should monitor the ongoing suitability of this designation and revise as appropriate. This allows the CIO to define a rules-based manner to select representatives such members of the CIO's office, or a bureau CIO, to represent the CIO for portions of the Common Baseline responsibilities described above (such as for contract review of purchases of less than a certain dollar threshold).

Agencies which plan to use such a rules-based method must describe it in a "CIO Assignment Plan" (Plan) and submit it for OMB approval as detailed in Section B above. Plans must show evidence that the CIO retains accountability for the designated alternative agency officials' involvement and decisions and that the appropriate level of rigor shall be executed by this official in place of the CIO. The agency shall post the Plan publicly at agency.gov/digitalstrategy and include it as a downloadable dataset in the agency's Public Data Listing not more than 30 days following the Plan's approval by OMB.

Legal text of FITARA: *"A covered agency… may use the governance processes of the agency to approve such a contract or other agreement if the Chief Information Officer of the agency is included as a full participant in the governance processes." Also, "[t]he head of each agency shall ensure that the Chief Information Officer of the agency has a significant role in… the decision processes for all annual and multi-year planning, programming, budgeting, and execution decisions, related reporting requirements, and reports related to IT and …the management, governance and oversight processes related to [IT]."*
40 U.S.C. § 11319(b)(1)(A) and (C)(i)(III)

Summary of Common Baseline for IT Management

Common Baseline for IT Management

CIO ASSIGNMENT PLAN (optional)

Section / *Responsibility*	Budget Formulation	Budget Execution	Acquisition	Organization & Workforce
Visibility	A1: Visibility of IT resource plans/decisions to CIO A2: Visibility of IT resource plans/decisions in budget materials	F1, F2: Visibility of IT expenditures reporting to CIO		
Planning	B1,B2. CIO role in pre-budget submission for programs C1,C2: CIO role in planning program management		I1: Shared acquisition and procurement responsibilities	P1,P2: IT Workforce planning
Governance		H1,H2: CIO role on program governance boards F2: Participate with CIO on governance boards J1. CIO role in modification, termination, or pause of IT G1: CIO defines IT processes and policies	K2: CAO is responsible for ensuring contract actions which require IT are consistent with CIO-approved plans and strategies I1,I2: Shared acquisition and procurement responsibilities	Q1: CIO reports to agency head (or to Deputy/COO)
Program Collaboration		E1,E2: Ongoing CIO engagement with program managers		N1,N2: CIO role in ongoing bureau CIOs' evaluations O1,O2: Bureau IT leadership Directory
Certifications & Approvals	D1, D2: CIO reviews and approves major IT investment portion of budget request	L1,L2: CIO approval of reprogramming requests	K1. CIO review and approval of acquisition strategy and acquisition plan.	M1: CIO approval of new bureau CIOs

Attachment B. Definitions of Terms for Purposes of this Guidance

Agency CIO	The Chief Information Officer at the headquarters level of a department or establishment of the government as defined in Section 20 of OMB Circular A-11 *(contrast with 'bureau CIO')*.
Bureau CIO	Official with the title or role of Chief Information Officer within a principal subordinate organizational unit of the agency, as defined in Section 20 of OMB Circular A-11, or any component organization of the agency *(contrast with 'agency CIO')*.
Major IT Investment	An IT investment requiring special management attention because of its importance to the mission or function to the government; significant program or policy implications; high executive visibility; high development, operating, or maintenance costs; unusual funding mechanism; or definition as major by the agency's capital planning and investment control process. Agencies should also include all "major automated information system" as defined in 10 U.S.C. 2445 and all "major acquisitions" as defined in the OMB Circular A-11 Capital Programming Guide consisting of information resources. OMB may work with the agency to declare IT investments as major IT investments. Agencies must consult with assigned OMB desk officers and resource management offices (RMOs) regarding which investments are considered "major." Investments not considered "major" are "non-major."
Reprogramming	Any movement of funds for IT resources that requires Congressional notification.
Adequate Incremental Development	For development of software or services, planned and actual delivery of new or modified technical functionality to users occurs at least every six months.
Information Technology	As described in Section A above: A. Any services or equipment, or interconnected system(s) or subsystem(s) of equipment, that are used in the automatic acquisition, storage, analysis, evaluation, manipulation, management, movement, control, display, switching, interchange, transmission, or reception of data or information by the agency; where B. such services or equipment are 'used by an agency' if used by the agency directly or if used by a contractor under a contract with the agency that requires either use of the services or equipment or requires use of the services or equipment to a significant extent in the performance of a service or the furnishing of a product. C. The term "information technology" includes computers, ancillary equipment (including imaging peripherals, input, output, and storage devices necessary for security and surveillance), peripheral equipment designed to be controlled by the central processing unit of a computer, software, firmware and similar procedures, services (including provisioned services such as cloud computing and support services that support any point of the lifecycle of the equipment or service), and related resources. D. The term "information technology" does not include any equipment that is acquired by a contractor incidental to a contract that does not require use of the equipment.
IT Resources	As described in Section A above: All agency budgetary resources, personnel, equipment, facilities, or services that are primarily used in the management, operation, acquisition, disposition, and transformation, or other activity related to the lifecycle of information technology; acquisitions or interagency agreements that include information technology and the services or equipment provided by such acquisitions or interagency agreements; but does not include grants to third parties which establish or support information technology not operated directly by the Federal Government.
"Shadow IT" or "Hidden IT"	Refers to spending on IT that is not fully transparent to the agency CIO and/or IT resources included as a portion of a program that is not primarily of an "information technology" purpose but delivers IT capabilities or contains IT resources. For example, a grants program that contains a portion of its spending on equipment, systems, or services that provide IT capabilities for administering or delivering the grants.
Contract	A mutually binding legal relationship obligating the seller to furnish the supplies or services (including construction) and the buyer to pay for them. It includes all types of commitments that obligate the Government to an expenditure of appropriated funds and that, except as otherwise authorized, are in writing. In addition to bilateral instruments, contracts include (but are not limited to) awards and notices of awards; job orders or task letters issued under basic ordering agreements; letter contracts; orders, such as purchase orders, under which the contract becomes effective by written acceptance or performance; and bilateral contract modifications. Contracts do not include grants and cooperative agreements covered by 31 U.S.C. § 6301, *et seq.* For discussion of various types of contracts, see Part 16. – FAR definitions

Attachment C: Template for Agency Common Baseline Self-Assessment and Plan

OMB will issue revised IDC reporting instructions that describe how agencies shall submit their self-assessment and plan using the below template or another template approved by OMB. Each element of the Common Baseline will be evaluated, along with accompanying evidence and steps to close the incompletely addressed areas.

	Overall Rating (1-3)*	Agency Explanation for Overall Rating	Agency Action Plans (provide for ratings of 1 & 2)	Agency Evidence of Complete Implementation (provide for ratings of 3)
		Budget Formulation and Planning. FITARA: "The CIO has a significant role in the decision processes for all annual and multi-year planning, programming, budgeting, and execution decisions."		
A				
B				
C				
D				
		Acquisition and Execution. FITARA: "The CIO has a significant role in the decision processes for all annual and multi-year planning, programming, budgeting, and execution decisions; management, governance and oversight processes related to IT; and certifies that IT investments are adequately implementing incremental development as defined in OMB capital planning guidance."		
E				
F				
G				

*Overall Ratings Defined –
1: Incomplete – Agency has not started development of a plan describing the changes it will make to ensure that all baseline FITARA responsibilities are in place by December 31, 2015.
2: Partially Addressed – Agency is working to develop a plan describing the changes it will make to ensure that all baseline FITARA responsibilities are in place by December 31, 2015.
3: Fully Implemented – Agency has developed and implemented its plan to ensure that all common baseline FITARA responsibilities are in place.

	Overall Rating (1-3)*	Agency Explanation for Overall Rating	Agency Action Plans (provide for ratings of 1 & 2)	Agency Evidence of Complete Implementation (provide for ratings of 3)
H				
I				
J				
K				
L				

Organization and Workforce. FITARA: "The CIO reports to the agency head (or deputy/COO) and assesses the requirements established for agency personnel regarding knowledge and skill in information resources management and the adequacy of those requirements for facilitating the achievement of the established IRM performance goals; and assesses the extent to which the positions and personnel at the executive and management levels meet those requirements."

	Overall Rating (1-3)*	Agency Explanation for Overall Rating	Agency Action Plans (provide for ratings of 1 & 2)	Agency Evidence of Complete Implementation (provide for ratings of 3)
M				
N				
O				
P				
Q				

*Overall Ratings Defined --
1: Incomplete – Agency has not started development of a plan describing the changes it will make to ensure that all baseline FITARA responsibilities are in place by December 31, 2015.
2: Partially Addressed – Agency is working to develop a plan describing the changes it will make to ensure that all baseline FITARA responsibilities are in place by December 31, 2015.
3: Fully Implemented – Agency has developed and implemented its plan to ensure that all common baseline FITARA responsibilities are in place.

Attachment D: Fiscal Year (FY) 2015 PortfolioStat

This Attachment describes changes to the PortfolioStat process used in FY 2015, including reporting requirements for agencies. This attachment also describes the goals and topics which agencies and OMB will address through the FY2015 PortfolioStat process.

PortfolioStat[25] was established in FY 2012 to assess the maturity of Federal IT portfolio management, consolidate and eliminate duplicative spending on Commodity IT,[26] and improve agency processes to drive mission and customer-focused IT solutions. PortfolioStat is an evidence-based, data-driven review of agency IT portfolio management with agency leadership that continues to drive significant cost savings and efficiencies. To date, agencies have saved over $2.59 billion,[27] exceeding the $2.5 billion in savings opportunities identified in the original FY 2012 PortfolioStat sessions.

Each year this process has evolved to better align Federal IT policy goals to agency IT portfolios. As part of this evolution, starting in FY 2015 we have changed PortfolioStat from being an annual review session to quarterly reviews. OMB now collects agency progress data on a quarterly basis[28] and as such has an obligation to provide timely performance feedback throughout the year. Sharing this feedback quarterly will better allow OMB to track progress and recommend course corrections more frequently.

In alignment with the Administration's core IT objectives, PortfolioStat sessions will focus on three key areas: (1) driving value in Federal IT investments, (2) delivering world-class digital services, and (3) protecting Federal IT assets and information. Prior to each quarterly PortfolioStat session, agencies will be provided a scorecard including agency-specific performance metric data (see *Fiscal Year 2015 PortfolioStat Performance Metrics* below for specific metrics) and portfolio analysis agenda items.

1. The agenda of PortfolioStat sessions between OMB and agencies will focus on the following initiatives:

   - **PortfolioStat Action Items.** Agencies will discuss the status of each PortfolioStat action item reported through the IDC with OMB.

   - **High Impact Programs.** Agencies will use *Attachment E: Investment and Portfolio Management Maturity Framework* to describe the strategy, progress, critical milestones, risk, and expected impact of investments included in High Impact Programs. OMB will continue to work with agencies to designate investments included in High Impact Programs.

   - **Agency Digital Service Teams and United States Digital Service (USDS).** OMB will review the agency's progress in laying the organizational groundwork and establishing Digital Service Teams, the agency's plan for effectively leveraging those resources, and the status of the performance of USDS activities.

---

[25] See OMB M-12-10, M-13-09, and M-14-08. PortfolioStat is a tool that agencies use to assess the current maturity of their IT portfolio management process, using data and analytics to make decisions on eliminating duplication, augment current CIO-led capital planning and investment control processes, and move to shared solutions in order to maximize the return on IT investments across the portfolio.

[26] See OMB M-11-29 *CIO Authorities* memorandum

[27] The Consolidated and Further Continuing Appropriations Act, 2015 (P.L. 113-235), includes an appropriation for the Office of Management and Budget to administer the Information Technology Oversight and Reform fund and requires the submission of quarterly reports "identifying the savings achieved by the Office of Management and Budget's governmentwide information technology reform efforts" with the "savings identified by fiscal year, agency and appropriation."

[28] See OMB M-13-09. This information is collected through the Integrated Data Collection (IDC) established in FY 2013 PortfolioStat. Quarterly IDC deadlines are the last days in May, August, November and February.

- **Commodity IT.** Agencies will discuss how they use category management[29] to consolidate commodity IT assets, eliminate duplication between assets, and improve procurement and management of hardware, software, network, and telecom services. Furthermore, agencies will share lessons-learned related to commodity IT procurement policies and efforts to establish enterprise-wide inventories of related information.

- **IT Management Roles and Responsibilities.** Agencies will discuss the status of their plans to implement the Common Baseline (*Attachment A*) and monitor the effectiveness of the CIO's execution of the included roles and responsibilities. This should include discussion of the CIO's relationship with other Senior Agency Officials, as well as those officials' execution of listed roles and responsibilities.

- **Portfolio Management Maturity.** Agencies will use the categories described in *Attachment E: Investment and Portfolio Management Maturity Framework* to evaluate the maturity of the agency's People, Technology, Governance, Process, and Acquisition capabilities related to IT resources. Agencies should describe how their policies implement the portfolio management, capital planning, and other processes required in OMB Circular A-130, OMB Circular A-11's capital planning and investment control guidance, and other OMB IT management policies, including this guidance. For example, agencies should describe how agency priority goals, agency strategic objectives, the IT investment portfolio, the Information Resource Management (IRM) Strategic Plan, and the Enterprise Roadmap relate to each other and support the efficient and effective accomplishment of agency program and business objectives. Finally, agencies should describe how they select the system development lifecycle frameworks used in IT development activities, such as the use of incremental development and modular approaches prioritized by customer requirements.

- **Data Center, Cloud, and Shared Services Optimization.** Agencies will discuss their progress using cloud computing and shared services to optimize data center activities and achieve overall IT objectives. This includes a discussion of how the agency is using FedRAMP services and ensuring cloud services meet applicable FISMA requirements.

- **Cybersecurity.** In addition to the "Protect" metrics in *Fiscal Year 2015 PortfolioStat Performance Metrics* below, PortfolioStat discussions will draw on topics covered in each agency's quarterly Cybersecurity Self-Assessments.

- **World-Class Customer Service.** Agencies shall discuss how their portfolio management practices emphasize the customer-centric themes of the U.S. Digital Services Playbook,[30] OMB's capital planning and investment control guidance,[31] and the Smarter IT Cross-Agency Priority (CAP) Goal.[32] Agencies should describe where in their policies the following are implemented: the Playbook's "Understand what people need" play, the capital planning guidance requirement for major investments to measure customer satisfaction performance metrics, and the Smarter IT CAP Goal's focus on improving outcomes and customer satisfaction with Federal services.

---

[29] See the OMB Office of Federal Procurement Policy *Transforming the Marketplace* (December 4, 2014) memorandum available at: https://www.whitehouse.gov/sites/default/files/omb/procurement/memo/simplifying-federal-procurement-to-improve-performance-drive-innovation-increase-savings.pdf.

[30] *U.S. Digital Services Playbook*, available at: https://playbook.cio.gov/.

[31] IT Budget Capital Planning Guidance available at: https://www.whitehouse.gov/omb/e-gov/strategiesandguides.

[32] *Smarter IT Delivery Cross-Agency Priority Goal*, available at: http://www.performance.gov/node/3403?view=public#overview.

- **Open Data.** Experts have calculated that the potential economic benefits of open data are in the trillions of dollars.[33] The Federal government has made significant strides in opening up data to drive economic growth. Currently there are over 117,000 data sets available on data.gov. As a next step, agencies should improve the quality and types of datasets. Agencies should continue to evaluate their enterprise data inventory, conduct outreach to understand the users of their data, improve customer feedback mechanisms, and release datasets—subject to privacy, confidentiality, security, or other valid restrictions.

- **Streamlining reporting.** OMB will continue to seek opportunities to reduce agency burden through revising reporting requirements and improving reporting channels through the ITDB and IDC as well as work with agencies to develop opportunities to improve the timeliness and reliability of reported ITDB data.

2. Quarterly PortfolioStat activities will take place in three phases: (1) Preparation; (2) Session; and (3) Post-Session. The following provides details on each phase with guidance on the schedule and requirements to ensure PortfolioStat is consistently implemented.

- **Phase 1: Preparation.** Following each quarterly agency IDC submission, OMB will analyze the latest data, consider trends in performance metrics over time, and review past PortfolioStat topics and PortfolioStat action items to identify topics for the upcoming PortfolioStat session's discussion. OMB will send these topics, analysis, and proposed agenda for each agency to the agency's PortfolioStat lead. Agencies are encouraged to work closely with OMB to provide clarifications and improvements to the preparation prior to the quarterly PortfolioStat session.

- **Phase 2: Session.** Agency PortfolioStat leads shall work with OMB to schedule a PortfolioStat session to be held within eight weeks following the relevant IDC quarter's submission deadline. In the session, OMB and the agency CIO will review updates to the agency's Strategic IRM Plan and Enterprise Roadmap, trending data from the agency's IDC and IT Dashboard submissions, discuss preceding quarterly PortfolioStat action items, status of investments included in High Impact Program(s), and select performance metrics.

  Based on the discussion, OMB and the agency will identify and agree on PortfolioStat action items (with specific deadlines) which OMB will send to the agency within two weeks of the completed session. Where appropriate, results from these sessions shall be integrated into agency budget submissions and Congressional Budget Justifications.

- **Phase 3: Post-Session.** Upon receipt of PortfolioStat action items, agency PortfolioStat leads shall work with OMB to include updates on the status of these items in the next quarterly PortfolioStat. Agencies that do not meet a deadline identified in a PortfolioStat action item shall brief the Federal CIO and the agency head at least once per quarter until the action item is complete.

  Agencies shall describe progress implementing each PortfolioStat action item as a part of quarterly IDC reporting. At least once per year, agency heads shall review with the agency CIO and certify that the reported status of each PortfolioStat action item is accurate and send this certification to OMB.

---

[33] *Open data: Unlocking innovation and performance with liquid information* (McKinsey & Company, October 2013) available at: http://www.mckinsey.com/insights/business_technology/open_data_unlocking_innovation_and_performance_with_liquid_information

Fiscal Year 2015 PortfolioStat Performance Metrics[34]

Category	Metric	Metric Definition
Drive Value in Federal IT Investments	Deliver on Budget	Percent of IT projects within 10% of budgeted cost (% "Green" cost variance on the IT Dashboard)
	Deliver on Schedule	Percent of IT projects within 10% of budgeted schedule (% "Green" schedule variance on the IT Dashboard)
	Development, Modernization, and Enhancement (DME) Spending	Percent of IT spending that is DME or provisioned services spending (DME normal + DME provisioned services + operations & maintenance provisioned services spending)
	IPv6 Adoption	Percent of operational "Internet Protocol version 6" (IPv6) enabled domains
	Commodity IT Spending	Infrastructure spending per person
Deliver World Class Services	Planned Delivery versus Actual Delivery	Average planned duration and average actual duration of completed activities providing key deliverables, usable functionality, iterative release, or production release for activities completed within the last year.
	Incremental or Agile Development	Average planned duration of future, in-progress, and completed activities providing key deliverables, usable functionality, iterative releases, or production releases by start year.
	Open Data Leading Indicators	Performance on Project Open Data Dashboard[35] leading indicators
	DAP Script Installed	Percent of second-level domains with the Digital Analytics Program (DAP) script installed
	Potential Mobile Savings	Estimated savings the agency could achieve in mobile device contracts as estimated by the GSA FSSI Economic Model
Protect Federal IT Assets and Information[36]	Information Security Continuous Monitoring (ISCM)	Average percentage of IT assets subject to an automated inventory, configuration, or vulnerability management capability.
	Identity Credential and Access Management (ICAM)	Percentage of all users required to use a Personal Identity Verification (PIV) card to authenticate to the agency network.
	FedRAMP Implementation	Percentage of Authorities to Operate (ATOs) that are FedRAMP[37] compliant[38].
	Security Incidents	Number of information security incidents reported to the United States Computer Emergency Readiness Team (US-CERT), by type.

---

[34] These metrics will be available on MAX and any future updates to performance metrics will be published there.

[35] Project Open Data Dashboard available at: http://labs.data.gov/dashboard/offices.

[36] Protect metrics are each based on a component of the Cybersecurity Cross-Agency Priority Goal described on Performance.gov. Each of these components is described in detail at: http://www.dhs.gov/xlibrary/assets/nppd/ciofismametricsfinal.pdf. The Cybersecurity CAP goal metrics are currently being revised for FY 2015 and therefore the performance metrics in this area are subject to change.

[37] Memorandum for Chief Information Officers: *Security Authorization of Information Systems in Cloud Computing Environments* (December 8, 2011).

[38] FedRAMP Compliant Systems: https://www.fedramp.gov/marketplace/compliant-systems/.

Attachment E: Investment and Portfolio Management Maturity Framework

When conducting TechStat reviews, PortfolioStat reviews, or evaluating investments related to High Impact Programs, agencies shall use the following framework for describing investment and portfolio management maturity with OMB. These scores may be compared or aggregated across bureaus, agencies, or governmentwide to provide a summary of overall IT management maturity. This model may be updated over time as common root causes of implementation challenges or other common management issues are identified. More details describing how to evaluate each area as Level 1, Level 2, or Level 3 will be provided as a part of the PortfolioStat process.

MANAGEMENT

	LEVEL 1 - REACTING	LEVEL 2 - IMPLEMENTING	LEVEL 3 - OPTIMIZING
Program/Project Management			
Portfolio Management			
Enterprise Strategy			
Financial Management			

PEOPLE

	LEVEL 1 - REACTING	LEVEL 2 - IMPLEMENTING	LEVEL 3 - OPTIMIZING
Leadership			
Accountability			
Talent/HRM			
Customer-Centric			

PROCESS

	LEVEL 1 - REACTING	LEVEL 2 - IMPLEMENTING	LEVEL 3 - OPTIMIZING
Governance			
Agile			
Transparency			
Complexity			

TECHNOLOGY

	LEVEL 1 - REACTING	LEVEL 2 - IMPLEMENTING	LEVEL 3 - OPTIMIZING
Security			
Scalability			
Open			
Reuse			

ACQUISITION

	LEVEL 1 - REACTING	LEVEL 2 - IMPLEMENTING	LEVEL 3 - OPTIMIZING
Strategic Sourcing			
Flexibility			
Scope			
Lock-in			

Attachment F: Additional Agency Human Capital Plan Requirements

In February 2015, OMB added the following additional requirements for civilian CFO Act agencies to those established in *Acquisition Workforce Development Strategic Plan for Civilian Agencies – FY2010 – 2014.*[39]

Additional FITARA Related Sections for Agency Human Capital Plan
IT Acquisition Cadres: Has your agency developed an information technology (IT) acquisition cadre or used a memoranda of understanding with other agencies that have such cadres or personnel with experience relevant to your agency's IT acquisition needs?   Select Yes or No If yes, please elaborate. If no, please explain your agency's plans for developing an IT acquisition cadre or explain why you are not developing an IT acquisition cadre.
Personnel Development: Has your agency taken steps to develop personnel assigned to IT acquisitions, including cross-functional training of acquisition IT and program personnel?   Select Yes or No If yes, please elaborate. If no, please explain if and how your agency plans to develop personnel assigned to IT acquisitions.
Specialized Career Path for IT Program Managers: Has your agency utilized the specialized career path for IT program managers as designated by OPM?   Select Yes or No Has your agency strengthened IT program management?   Select Yes or No If yes, how many IT program managers have you designated? If no, does your agency plan to utilize the specialized career path? When? If your agency has strengthened IT program management, please explain how it has done so. If your agency has not strengthened IT program management yet, please explain if it plans to do so and how. If it is not planning to strengthen IT program management, please explain why.
Direct Hire Authority: Has your agency utilized direct hire authority relating to personnel assigned to IT acquisitions?   Select Yes or No If yes, how many times and for what job series has your agency utilized direct hire authority in this area. If no, please explain your agency's plans to utilize direct hire authority in this area or explain why it does not plan to use this authority.
Peer Reviews: Has your agency conducted peer reviews of IT acquisitions?   Select Yes or No If yes, please elaborate on the number and types of IT acquisitions reviewed. If no, please explain your agency's plans to conduct peer reviews of IT acquisition or explain why it does not plan to conduct peer reviews of IT acquisitions.
Pilot Programs: Has your agency utilized pilot programs of innovative approaches to developing the IT acquisition workforce, such as industry-government rotations?   Select Yes or No If yes, please explain what pilot program you have used or are using. If no, please explain your agency's plans to utilize pilot programs of innovative approaches to developing the IT acquisition workforce or why it does not plan to utilize these programs.

---

[39] Available online at: http://www.whitehouse.gov/sites/default/files/omb/assets/procurement_workforce/AWF_Plan_10272009.pdf

Attachment G: Related Forthcoming Policies Roadmap

Some requirements and objectives described throughout this document are related to forthcoming new policies or changes to existing guidance/instructions to be released later in FY2015, such as:

		Legislative Requirements Addressed	Estimated Timeframe
1	Updates to OMB Circular A-130: Management of Federal Information Resources	FISMA Modernization, overall IT management, governance and role of CIO, privacy, and information management	December 2015
2	A-11 budget preparation requirements: – CIO/CFO statements in overall budget submission (OMB Justification) (Sections 25, 31, 51.3) – Section 55 capital planning and investment control reporting requirements (formerly Exhibit 53 and Exhibit 300)	FITARA Section 831: CIO Authorities	June 2015
3	E-Gov Integrated Data Collection (IDC) reporting instructions	Reporting requirements throughout FITARA	June 2015 (New instructions to be published)
4	FITARA-related FSSI FAR case	FITARA Section 836: FSSI	Opened February 2015, completion estimated in FY2016
5	OMB Circular A-123: Management's Responsibility for Internal Controls • Inclusion of IT management in material weaknesses identified in annual assurance statement.	FITARA Section 831: CIO Authorities	June 2015
6	Data Center Optimization Policy	FITARA Section 834: Data Center Consolidation	By end of FY2015

Attachment H: Cross-Walk of FITARA Requirements

The materials below summarize which portions of the above guidance address which sections of
FITARA.

		Section of Legislation	Section of Guidance
1. CIO Authorities			
	Contract review	Section 831: CIO Authority Enhancements Subsection (b)(1)(C)(i)(I)	Page 4: Implementation of the Common Baseline Page 12: *Attachment A* (F1)
	Reprogramming review	Section 831: Subsection (b)(1)(C)(i)(II)	Page 4 and Page 11 (B1)
	Adequate incremental development	Section 831: Subsection (b)(1)(B)(ii)	Page 4 and Page 14 (M1)
	Budget approval	Section 831: Subsection (b)(1)(B)(i)	Page 4 and Page 11 (A1, C1)
	Bureau CIO approval	Section 831: Subsection (b)(2)	Page 4 and Page 14-15 (N1, O1)
	Other responsibilities	Section 831: Subsection (b)(1)(C)(i)(III) Subsection (b)(1)(A)(i) Subsection (b)(1)(A)(ii)	Page 4 and Pages 11-17
2. Transparency			
2A	Federal IT Dashboard	Section 832: Enhanced Transparency and Improved Risk Management in Information Technology Investments Subsection (3)(3)(A)	Page 6: Transparency, Risk Management, Portfolio Review, and Reporting
2B	Agency IT Dashboard data	Section 832: Subsection (3)(3)(B)(i)	Page 6
2B1	CIO Evaluations Guidance from OMB	Section 832: Subsection (3)(3)(B)(i)	Page 6
2B2	IT Dashboard Data Must Be Provided Bi-Annually	Section 832: Subsection (3)(3)(B)(ii)	Page 6
2B3	Required Agency/Project Data Improvement Programs	Section 832: Subsection (3)(3)(D)	Page 6
2C	TechStat Trigger	Section 832: Subsection (4)	Page 7
2C1	TechStat Topics	Section 832: Subsection (4)(A)	Page 7
2C2	OMB TechStat Reporting to Congress	Section 832: Subsection (4)(B)	Page 7
2C3	DME Freeze One Year Post TechStat	Section 832: Subsection (4)(D)	Page 7
3. Portfolio Reviews			
3	**PortfolioStat**	Section 833: Portfolio Review Subsection (c)(1)	Page 7: Transparency, Risk Management, Portfolio Review, and Reporting
3A	PortfolioStat Process Requirements	Section 833: Subsection (c)(1)	Page 7 and Page 21-24 *Attachment D*: FY2015 PortfolioStat
3B	PortfolioStat Metrics, Cost Savings, and Avoidance	Section 833: Subsection (c)(2)	Page 7-8 and *Attachment D*
3C	PortfolioStat Annual Review	Section 833: Subsection (c)(3)	Page 8 and *Attachment D*
3E	Quarterly Reports	Section 833: Subsection (c)(5)	Page 8 and *Attachment D*

4. Data Center Consolidation Section

	FDCCI	Section 834: Federal Data Center Consolidation Initiative	Page 8: Federal Data Center Consolidation Initiative (FDCCI)
	Agency Reporting	Section 834(b)(1)(A)	Page 8
	Agency Annual Inventory	Section 834(b)(1)(A)(i)	To be addressed in forthcoming guidance and/or IDC instructions
	Agency Annual Strategy	Section 834(b)(1)(A)(ii)	To be addressed in forthcoming guidance and/or IDC instructions
	Agency Annual Statement	Section 834(b)(1)(D)	To be addressed in forthcoming guidance and/or IDC instructions
	Agency Quarterly Updates	Section 834(b)(1)(E)(i)(II)	Page 8
	OMB Reporting and Requirements	Section 834(b)(2)	To be addressed in forthcoming guidance and/or IDC instructions
	GAO Review	Section 834(b)(4)	Not specified
	Cybersecurity and Cloud Computing	Section 834(c)	Not specified

5-7. Acquisition/Procurement Sections

	IT Acquisition Cadres	Section 835: Expansion of Training and Use of Information Technology Cadres	Page 9: Information Technology Acquisition Requirements
	FSSI Strategic Sourcing	Section 836: Maximizing the Benefit of the Federal Strategic Sourcing Initiative	Page 9: Information Technology Acquisition Requirements
	Governmentwide Software Purchasing Program	Section 837: Governmentwide Software Purchasing Program	Page 9: Information Technology Acquisition Requirements

Attachment I: Summary of Agency Deadlines and Requirements

Topic	Requirement	Deadline
Common Baseline for IT Management	Agencies which operate systems related to national security	Meet with OMB within 60 days following the final release of the guidance to discuss requirements
	Complete agency self-assessment and plan, as well as CIO Assignment Plan, if used, and submit to OMB for approval	By August 15, 2015
	Publish agency implementation plan and CIO Assignment Plan to the agency's public website and include in public data listing	Within 30 days of receiving OMB approval of plan
	Publicly publish Bureau IT Leadership Directory as a dataset in public data listing as instructed in IDC	List in agency public data listing by August 15, 2015 and kept up to date thereafter
	IT processes and policies publicly posted at agency.gov/digitalstrategy and include as a dataset in public data listing as instructed in IDC	By August 30, 2015 and kept up to date thereafter
	OMB shall be notified of all governance boards the CIO is a member of via IDC	By August 30, 2015 and kept up to date thereafter via IDC
	Include IT statements regarding CIO involvement in budget formulation (see OMB Circular A-11 for FY2017)	September 2015 with preliminary budget materials
	Agency-wide critical element(s) included in all bureau CIOs' performance evaluations	By December 31, 2015
	Adopt Common Baseline	By December 31, 2015
	Conduct annual agency review and update self-assessment	By April 30, 2016 and each April on an annual basis
IT Dashboard (Enhanced Transparency)	Monthly reporting to IT Dashboard	As data are available, or at least once per calendar month for each major IT investment
	Data improvement program	Address unreliable or untimely IT Dashboard data within 30 days; provide status update as a part of quarterly IDC
TechStat (Improved Risk Management)	Notify OMB of Planned TechStat Session	At least 2 weeks in advance via email

	Automatic TechStat sessions for high risk rated investments (three months)	Within 30 days of the completion of the third month where CIO evaluation is "Red" ("three months" begins July 1, 2015)
	Report TechStat outcomes and outputs	Via IDC
	Automatic OMB performance and budgetary actions	Completion of four consecutive quarters where CIO evaluation is still "Red" following an automatic TechStat (beginning July 1, 2015)
PortfolioStat (Portfolio Review)	PortfolioStat Sessions	Quarterly: Within 8 weeks following the IDC submission deadline
	Agency receives PortfolioStat action items from OMB	Within 2 weeks of PortfolioStat session
	Agencies send updates on status of action items	Quarterly via IDC
	Agency heads review and certify the status of PortfolioStat action items with the agency CIO and send certification to OMB	Annually via IDC
	Agencies brief Federal CIO and agency head on status of action items which have missed a deadline until complete.	Quarterly following a missed deadline
IT Acquisition Requirements	Continued submission of Acquisition Workforce Development Strategic Plans	April 15, 2015, and annually thereafter

Attachment J: Common Acronyms and Abbreviations

ASAM	Assistant Secretaries for Management
ATO	Authority to Operate
CAO	Chief Acquisition Officer
CAP Goal	Cross Agency Priority Goal
CFO	Chief Financial Officer
CFO Act	Chief Financial Officer Act of 1990
CHCO	Chief Human Capital Officer
CIO	Chief Information Officer
COO	Chief Operating Officer
COSH	Cost per Operating System per Hour
CPIC	Capital Planning and Investment Control
CXO	Senior Agency Official such as CAO, CFO, CHCO, CIO, COO
DAP	Digital Analytics Program
DME	Development, Modernization, and Enhancement
ECQ	Executive Core Qualifications
E-Gov	Office of E-Government and Information Technology
FAC-PPM	Federal Acquisition Certification for Program and Project Managers
FAR	Federal Acquisition Regulation
FAR Council	Federal Acquisition Regulatory Council
FDCCI	Federal Data Center Consolidation Initiative
FISMA	Federal Information Security Management Act/Federal Information Security Modernization Act
FITARA	Federal Information Technology Acquisition Reform Act
FSSI	Federal Strategic Sourcing Initiative
FTE	Full Time Equivalent
FY	Fiscal Year
GAO	Government Accountability Office
GSA	General Services Administration
GS	Grade Schedule
ICAM	Identity Credential and Access Management
IDC	Integrated Data Collection
IPv6	Internet Protocol version 6
IRB	Investment Review Board
IRM	Information Resource Management
ISCM	Information Security Continuous Monitoring
IT	Information Technology
ITDB	Federal IT Dashboard
NIST	National Institute for Standards and Technology
O&M	Operations and Maintenance
OFPP	Office of Federal Procurement Policy
OMB	Office of Management and Budget
OS	Operating System

PIV	Personal Identity Verification
PL	Public Law
PMC	President's Management Council
PUE	Power Usage Effectiveness
SAO	Senior Agency Official, as referred to in this guidance, includes positions such as the CFO, CHCO, CAO, ASAM, COOs, and Program Managers
SES	Senior Executive Service
SL	Senior Level
ST	Scientific or Professional Position
U.S.C.	United States Code
US-CERT	United States Computer Emergency Readiness Team
USDS	United States Digital Service

United States Government Accountability Office

Testimony before the Subcommittees on Government Operations and Information Technology, Committee on Oversight and Government Reform, House of Representatives

For Release on Delivery
Expected at 2:00 p.m. ET
Wednesday, November 15, 2017

INFORMATION TECHNOLOGY

Further Implementation of FITARA Related Recommendations Is Needed to Better Manage Acquisitions and Operations

Statement of David A. Powner, Director
Information Technology Management Issues

GAO Highlights

Highlights of GAO-18-234T, a testimony before the Subcommittees on Government Operations and Information Technology, Committee on Oversight and Government Reform, House of Representatives

INFORMATION TECHNOLOGY

Further Implementation of FITARA Related Recommendations Is Needed to Better Manage Acquisitions and Operations

Why GAO Did This Study

The federal government plans to invest almost $96 billion on IT in fiscal year 2018. Historically, these investments have too often failed, incurred cost overruns and schedule slippages, or contributed little to mission-related outcomes. Accordingly, in December 2014, Congress enacted FITARA, aimed at improving agencies' acquisitions of IT. Further, in February 2015, GAO added improving the management of IT acquisitions and operations to its high-risk list.

This statement summarizes agencies' progress in improving the management of IT acquisitions and operations. It is based on GAO's prior and recently published reports on (1) data center consolidation, (2) risk levels of major investments as reported on OMB's IT Dashboard, (3) implementation of incremental development practices, and (4) management of software licenses.

What GAO Recommends

From fiscal years 2010 through 2015, GAO made about 800 recommendations to OMB and federal agencies to address shortcomings in IT acquisitions and operations, and included recommendations to improve the oversight and execution of the data center consolidation initiative, the accuracy and reliability of the Dashboard, incremental development policies, and software license management. Most agencies agreed with GAO's recommendations and had taken some actions or had no comments. In addition, from fiscal year 2016 to present, GAO has made more than 200 new recommendations in this area. GAO will continue to monitor agencies' implementation of these recommendations.

View GAO-18-234T. For more information, contact David A. Powner at (202) 512-9286 or pownerd@gao.gov.

What GAO Found

The Office of Management and Budget (OMB) and federal agencies have taken steps to improve the management of information technology (IT) acquisitions and operations through a series of initiatives, and as of November 2017, had fully implemented about 56 percent of the approximately 800 related GAO recommendations made between fiscal years 2010 through 2015. However, important additional actions are needed.

- **Consolidating data centers**. OMB launched an initiative in 2010 to reduce data centers, which was reinforced by the Federal Information Technology Acquisition Reform Act (FITARA) in 2014. However, in a series of reports that GAO issued over the past 6 years, it noted that, while data center consolidation could potentially save the federal government billions of dollars, weaknesses existed in several areas, including agencies' data center consolidation plans, data center optimization, and OMB's tracking and reporting on related cost savings. These reports contained a matter for Congressional consideration, and a total of 160 recommendations to OMB and 24 agencies, to improve the execution and oversight of the initiative. Most agencies and OMB agreed with the recommendations or had no comments. As of November 2017, 84 of the recommendations remained open.
- **Enhancing transparency**. OMB's IT Dashboard provides information on major investments at federal agencies, including ratings from Chief Information Officers that should reflect the level of risk facing an investment. Over the past 6 years, GAO has issued a series of reports about the Dashboard that noted both significant steps OMB has taken to enhance the oversight, transparency, and accountability of federal IT investments by creating its Dashboard, as well as concerns about the accuracy and reliability of the data. In total, GAO has made 47 recommendations to OMB and federal agencies to help improve the accuracy and reliability of the information on the Dashboard and to increase its availability. Most agencies agreed with the recommendations or had no comments. As of November 2017, 25 of these recommendations remained open.
- **Implementing incremental development**. OMB has emphasized the need for agencies to deliver investments in smaller parts, or increments, in order to reduce risk and deliver capabilities more quickly. Since 2012, OMB has required investments to deliver functionality every 6 months. Further, GAO has issued reports highlighting additional actions needed by OMB and agencies to improve their implementation of incremental development. In these reports, GAO made 42 recommendations. Most agencies agreed or did not comment on the recommendations. As of November 2017, 34 of the recommendations remained open.
- **Managing software licenses**. Effective management of software licenses can help avoid purchasing too many licenses that result in unused software. In May 2014, GAO reported that better management of licenses was needed to achieve savings, and made 136 recommendations to improve such management. Most agencies generally agreed with the recommendations or had no comments. As of November 2017, 112 of the recommendations remained open.

_____ United States Government Accountability Office

Chairmen Meadows and Hurd, Ranking Members Connolly and Kelly, and Members of the Subcommittees:

I am pleased to be here today to provide an update on federal agencies' efforts to improve the acquisition of information technology (IT). As I have previously testified, the effective and efficient acquisition of IT has been a long-standing challenge in the federal government.[1] In particular, the federal government has spent billions of dollars on failed and poorly performing IT investments, which often suffered from ineffective management. Recognizing the importance of government-wide acquisition of IT, in December 2014, Congress enacted federal IT acquisition reform legislation (commonly referred to as the Federal Information Technology Acquisition Reform Act, or FITARA).[2]

In addition, in February 2015, we added improving the management of IT acquisitions and operations to our list of high-risk areas for the federal government.[3] We recently issued an update to our high-risk report and noted that, while progress has been made in addressing the high-risk area of IT acquisitions and operations, significant work remains to be completed.[4]

My statement today provides an update on agencies' progress in improving the management of IT acquisitions and operations. The statement is based on our prior and recently published reports that discuss federal agencies' (1) data center consolidation efforts, (2) risk levels of major investments as reported on OMB's IT Dashboard, (3) implementation of incremental development practices, and (4) management of software licenses. A more detailed discussion of the

---

[1]GAO, *Information Technology: Sustained Management Attention to the Implementation of FITARA Is Needed to Better Manage Acquisitions and Operations,* GAO-17-686T (Washington, D.C.: June 13, 2017).

[2]Carl Levin and Howard P. 'Buck' McKeon National Defense Authorization Act for Fiscal Year 2015, Pub. L. No. 113-291, div. A, title VIII, subtitle D, 128 Stat. 3292, 3438-3450 (Dec. 19, 2014).

[3]GAO, *High-Risk Series: An Update,* GAO-15-290 (Washington, D.C.: Feb. 11, 2015). GAO maintains a high-risk program to focus attention on government operations that it identifies as high risk due to their greater vulnerabilities to fraud, waste, abuse, and mismanagement or the need for transformation to address economy, efficiency, or effectiveness challenges.

[4]GAO, *High-Risk Series: Progress on Many High-Risk Areas, While Substantial Efforts Needed on Others,* GAO-17-317 (Washington, D.C.: Feb. 15, 2017).

objectives, scope, and methodology for this work is included in each of the reports that are cited throughout this statement.

We conducted the work upon which this statement is based in accordance with generally accepted government auditing standards. Those standards require that we plan and perform the audit to obtain sufficient, appropriate evidence to provide a reasonable basis for our findings and conclusions based on our audit objectives. We believe that the evidence obtained provides a reasonable basis for our findings and conclusions based on our audit objectives.

Background

According to the President's budget, the federal government plans to invest more than $96 billion for IT in fiscal year 2018—the largest amount ever. However, as we have previously reported, investments in federal IT too often result in failed projects that incur cost overruns and schedule slippages, while contributing little to the desired mission-related outcomes. For example:

- The Department of Veterans Affairs' Scheduling Replacement Project was terminated in September 2009 after spending an estimated $127 million over 9 years.[5]

- The tri-agency[6] National Polar-orbiting Operational Environmental Satellite System was halted in February 2010 by the White House's Office of Science and Technology Policy after the program spent 16 years and almost $5 billion.[7]

---

[5]GAO, *Information Technology: Management Improvements Are Essential to VA's Second Effort to Replace Its Outpatient Scheduling System,* GAO-10-579 (Washington, D.C.: May 27, 2010).

[6]The weather satellite program was managed by the National Oceanic and Atmospheric Administration, the Department of Defense, and the National Aeronautics and Space Administration.

[7]See, for example, GAO, *Polar-Orbiting Environmental Satellites: With Costs Increasing and Data Continuity at Risk, Improvements Needed in Tri-agency Decision Making,* GAO-09-564 (Washington, D.C.: June 17, 2009) and *Environmental Satellites: Polar-Orbiting Satellite Acquisition Faces Delays; Decisions Needed on Whether and How to Ensure Climate Data Continuity,* GAO-08-518 (Washington, D.C.: May 16, 2008).

- The Department of Homeland Security's Secure Border Initiative Network program was ended in January 2011, after the department obligated more than $1 billion for the program.[8]

- The Office of Personnel Management's Retirement Systems Modernization program was canceled in February 2011, after the agency had spent approximately $231 million on its third attempt to automate the processing of federal employee retirement claims.[9]

- The Department of Veterans Affairs' Financial and Logistics Integrated Technology Enterprise program was intended to be delivered by 2014 at a total estimated cost of $609 million, but was terminated in October 2011.[10]

- The Department of Defense's Expeditionary Combat Support System was canceled in December 2012 after spending more than a billion dollars and failing to deploy within 5 years of initially obligating funds.[11]

Our past work found that these and other failed IT projects often suffered from a lack of disciplined and effective management, such as project planning, requirements definition, and program oversight and governance. In many instances, agencies had not consistently applied best practices that are critical to successfully acquiring IT.

---

[8]See, for example, GAO, *Secure Border Initiative: DHS Needs to Strengthen Management and Oversight of Its Prime Contractor,* GAO-11-6 (Washington, D.C.: Oct. 18, 2010); *Secure Border Initiative: DHS Needs to Reconsider Its Proposed Investment in Key Technology Program,* GAO-10-340 (Washington, D.C.: May 5, 2010); and *Secure Border Initiative: DHS Needs to Address Testing and Performance Limitations That Place Key Technology Program at Risk,* GAO-10-158 (Washington, D.C.: Jan. 29, 2010).

[9]See, for example, GAO, *Office of Personnel Management: Retirement Modernization Planning and Management Shortcomings Need to Be Addressed,* GAO-09-529 (Washington, D.C.: Apr. 21, 2009) and *Office of Personnel Management: Improvements Needed to Ensure Successful Retirement Systems Modernization,* GAO-08-345 (Washington, D.C.: Jan. 31, 2008).

[10]GAO, *Information Technology: Actions Needed to Fully Establish Program Management Capability for VA's Financial and Logistics Initiative,* GAO-10-40 (Washington, D.C.: Oct. 26, 2009).

[11]GAO, *DOD Financial Management: Implementation Weaknesses in Army and Air Force Business Systems Could Jeopardize DOD's Auditability Goals,* GAO-12-134 (Washington, D.C.: Feb. 28, 2012) and *DOD Business Transformation: Improved Management Oversight of Business System Modernization Efforts Needed,* GAO-11-53 (Washington, D.C.: Oct. 7, 2010).

Such projects have also failed due to a lack of oversight and governance. Executive-level governance and oversight across the government has often been ineffective, specifically from chief information officers (CIO). For example, we have reported that some CIOs' roles were limited because they did not have the authority to review and approve the entire agency IT portfolio.[12]

Implementing FITARA Can Improve Agencies' Management of IT

FITARA was intended to improve agencies' acquisitions of IT and enable Congress to monitor agencies' progress and hold them accountable for reducing duplication and achieving cost savings. The law includes specific requirements related to seven areas.[13]

- **Federal data center consolidation initiative (FDCCI).** Agencies are required to provide OMB with a data center inventory, a strategy for consolidating and optimizing their data centers (to include planned cost savings), and quarterly updates on progress made. The law also requires OMB to develop a goal for how much is to be saved through this initiative, and provide annual reports on cost savings achieved.

- **Enhanced transparency and improved risk management.** OMB and covered agencies are to make detailed information on federal IT investments publicly available, and agency CIOs are to categorize their investments by level of risk. Additionally, in the case of major IT investments[14] rated as high risk for 4 consecutive quarters, the law requires that the agency CIO and the investment's program manager

---

[12]GAO, *Federal Chief Information Officers: Opportunities Exist to Improve Role in Information Technology Management*, GAO-11-634 (Washington, D.C.: Sept. 15, 2011).

[13]The provisions apply to the agencies covered by the Chief Financial Officers Act of 1990, 31 U.S.C. § 901(b). These agencies are the Departments of Agriculture, Commerce, Defense, Education, Energy, Health and Human Services, Homeland Security, Housing and Urban Development, Justice, Labor, State, the Interior, the Treasury, Transportation, and Veterans Affairs; the Environmental Protection Agency, General Services Administration, National Aeronautics and Space Administration, National Science Foundation, Nuclear Regulatory Commission, Office of Personnel Management, Small Business Administration, Social Security Administration, and U.S. Agency for International Development. However, FITARA has generally limited application to the Department of Defense.

[14]Major IT investment means a system or an acquisition requiring special management attention because it has significant program or policy implications; high executive visibility; high development, operating, or maintenance costs; an unusual funding mechanism; or is defined as major by the agency's capital planning and investment control process.

conduct a review aimed at identifying and addressing the causes of the risk.

- **Agency CIO authority enhancements.** CIOs at covered agencies are required to (1) approve the IT budget requests of their respective agencies, (2) certify that OMB's incremental development guidance is being adequately implemented for IT investments, (3) review and approve contracts for IT, and (4) approve the appointment of other agency employees with the title of CIO.

- **Portfolio review.** Agencies are to annually review IT investment portfolios in order to, among other things, increase efficiency and effectiveness and identify potential waste and duplication. In establishing the process associated with such portfolio reviews, the law requires OMB to develop standardized performance metrics, to include cost savings, and to submit quarterly reports to Congress on cost savings.

- **Expansion of training and use of IT acquisition cadres.** Agencies are to update their acquisition human capital plans to address supporting the timely and effective acquisition of IT. In doing so, the law calls for agencies to consider, among other things, establishing IT acquisition cadres or developing agreements with other agencies that have such cadres.

- **Government-wide software purchasing program.** The General Services Administration is to develop a strategic sourcing initiative to enhance government-wide acquisition and management of software. In doing so, the law requires that, to the maximum extent practicable, the General Services Administration should allow for the purchase of a software license agreement that is available for use by all executive branch agencies as a single user.[15]

- **Maximizing the benefit of the Federal Strategic Sourcing Initiative.**[16] Federal agencies are required to compare their purchases of services and supplies to what is offered under the

---

[15]The Making Electronic Government Accountable by Yielding Tangible Efficiencies Act of 2016, or the "MEGABYTE Act" further enhances CIOs' management of software licenses by requiring agency CIOs to establish an agency software licensing policy and a comprehensive software license inventory to track and maintain licenses, among other requirements. Pub. L. No. 114-210 (July 29, 2016); 130 Stat. 824.

[16]The Federal Strategic Sourcing Initiative is a program established by the General Services Administration and the Department of the Treasury to address government-wide opportunities to strategically source commonly purchased goods and services and eliminate duplication of efforts across agencies.

Federal Strategic Sourcing Initiative. OMB is also required to issue regulations related to the initiative.

In June 2015, OMB released guidance describing how agencies are to implement FITARA.[17] This guidance is intended to, among other things:

- assist agencies in aligning their IT resources with statutory requirements;

- establish government-wide IT management controls that will meet the law's requirements, while providing agencies with flexibility to adapt to unique agency processes and requirements;

- clarify the CIO's role and strengthen the relationship between agency CIOs and bureau CIOs; and

- strengthen CIO accountability for IT costs, schedules, performance, and security.

The guidance identified several actions that agencies were to take to establish a basic set of roles and responsibilities (referred to as the common baseline) for CIOs and other senior agency officials, which were needed to implement the authorities described in the law. For example, agencies were required to conduct a self-assessment and submit a plan describing the changes they intended to make to ensure that common baseline responsibilities were implemented. Agencies were to submit their plans to OMB's Office of E-Government and Information Technology by August 15, 2015, and make portions of the plans publicly available on agency websites no later than 30 days after OMB approval. As of November 2016, all agencies had made their plans publicly available.

In addition, in August 2016, OMB released guidance intended to, among other things, define a framework for achieving the data center consolidation and optimization requirements of FITARA.[18] The guidance includes requirements for agencies to:

- maintain complete inventories of all data center facilities owned, operated, or maintained by or on behalf of the agency;

---

[17]OMB, *Management and Oversight of Federal Information Technology*, Memorandum M-15-14 (Washington, D.C.: June 10, 2015).

[18]OMB, *Data Center Optimization Initiative (DCOI),* Memorandum M-16-19 (Washington D.C.: Aug. 1, 2016).

- develop cost savings targets for fiscal years 2016 through 2018 and report any actual realized cost savings; and

- measure progress toward meeting optimization metrics on a quarterly basis.

The guidance also directs agencies to develop a data center consolidation and optimization strategic plan that defines the agency's data center strategy for fiscal years 2016, 2017, and 2018. This strategy is to include, among other things, a statement from the agency CIO indicating whether the agency has complied with all data center reporting requirements in FITARA. Further, the guidance indicates that OMB is to maintain a public dashboard that will display consolidation-related costs savings and optimization performance information for the agencies.

IT Acquisitions and Operations Identified by GAO as a High-Risk Area

In February 2015, we introduced a new government-wide high-risk area, *Improving the Management of IT Acquisitions and Operations.*[19] This area highlighted several critical IT initiatives in need of additional congressional oversight, including (1) reviews of troubled projects; (2) efforts to increase the use of incremental development; (3) efforts to provide transparency relative to the cost, schedule, and risk levels for major IT investments; (4) reviews of agencies' operational investments; (5) data center consolidation; and (6) efforts to streamline agencies' portfolios of IT investments. We noted that implementation of these initiatives was inconsistent and more work remained to demonstrate progress in achieving IT acquisition and operation outcomes.

Further, our February 2015 high-risk report stated that, beyond implementing FITARA, OMB and agencies needed to continue to implement our prior recommendations in order to improve their ability to effectively and efficiently invest in IT. Specifically, from fiscal years 2010 through 2015, we made 803 recommendations to OMB and federal agencies to address shortcomings in IT acquisitions and operations. These recommendations included many to improve the implementation of the aforementioned six critical IT initiatives and other government-wide, cross-cutting efforts. We stressed that OMB and agencies should demonstrate government-wide progress in the management of IT investments by, among other things, implementing at least 80 percent of

---

[19]GAO-15-290.

our recommendations related to managing IT acquisitions and operations within 4 years.

In February 2017, we issued an update to our high-risk series and reported that, while progress had been made in improving the management of IT acquisitions and operations, significant work still remained to be completed.[20] For example, as of November 2017, OMB and agencies had fully implemented 452 (or about 56 percent) of the 803 recommendations. This was an increase of about 284 recommendations compared to the number of recommendations we reported as being fully implemented in 2015. Figure 1 summarizes the progress that OMB and agencies have made in addressing our recommendations as compared to the 80 percent target, as of November 2017.

Figure 1: Summary of the Office of Management and Budget's and Federal Agencies' Progress in Addressing GAO's Recommendations, as of November 2017

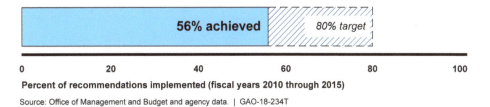

| 0 | 20 | 40 | 60 | 80 | 100 |

Percent of recommendations implemented (fiscal years 2010 through 2015)

Source: Office of Management and Budget and agency data. | GAO-18-234T

In addition, in fiscal year 2016, we made 202 new recommendations, thus further reinforcing the need for OMB and agencies to address the shortcomings in IT acquisitions and operations. Also, beyond addressing our prior recommendations, our 2017 high-risk update noted the importance of OMB and federal agencies continuing to expeditiously implement the requirements of FITARA.

To further explore the challenges and opportunities to improve federal IT acquisitions and operations, we convened a forum on September 14, 2016, to explore challenges and opportunities for CIOs to improve federal IT acquisitions and operations—with the goal of better informing policymakers and government leadership.[21] Forum participants, which included 13 current and former federal agency CIOs, members of Congress, and private sector IT executives, identified key actions related

---

[20]GAO-17-317.

[21]GAO, *Information Technology: Opportunities for Improving Acquisitions and Operations,* GAO-17-251SP (Washington, D.C.: Apr. 11, 2017).

to seven topics: (1) strengthening FITARA, (2) improving CIO authorities, (3) budget formulation, (4) governance, (5) workforce, (6) operations, and (7) transition planning. A summary of the key actions, by topic area, identified during the forum is provided in figure 2.

Figure 2: Key Actions, by Topic Area, Identified by Forum Participants to Improve Information Technology Acquisitions and Operations

STRENGTHENING FITARA'S IMPACT	• Congressional oversight could be more aggressive • Office of Management and Budget (OMB) may need to strengthen its role • The Department of Defense should be required to implement all provisions of the Federal Information Technology Acquisition Reform Act (FITARA)
IMPROVING CIO AUTHORITIES	• Have the Chief Information Officers (CIO) Council play an enhanced role in improving authorities • Implement collaborative governance • Evolve the role of the CIO to enable change • Focus on cybersecurity to change existing cultures
BUDGET FORMULATION	• Use information technology (IT) spend plans to improve budgets • Examine agency programs to capture additional IT spending • Simplify the definition of IT • Work more closely with procurement organizations • Work with congressional committees to explore budgeting flexibilities
GOVERNANCE	• Obtain support from agency leadership • Enhance governance at OMB and agencies • Use security authorities to enhance governance • Strengthen oversight for IT purchased as a service • Buy more and develop less • Evolve procurement processes to align with new technologies
WORKFORCE	• Attract more qualified CIOs by appealing to key missions • Have the Federal CIO play a more active role in attracting agency CIOs • Give CIOs more human resource flexibilities • Focus on attracting and investing in a more holistic IT workforce • Better integrate private sector talent into the IT workforce
OPERATIONS	• Use a strategic approach for legacy system migration • Migrate more services to the cloud • Implement strategies to mitigate the impact on jobs when closing data centers
TRANSITION PLANNING	• Convey IT and cyber issues early to leadership • Encourage Congress to focus on IT and cybersecurity at confirmation hearings • Ensure that IT and cyber issues are OMB priorities • Ensure GAO plays a role highlighting its work and expertise

Source: GAO analysis. | GAO-18-234T

In addition, in January 2017, the Federal CIO Council concluded that differing levels of authority over IT-related investments and spending have led to inconsistencies in how IT is executed from agency to agency. According to the Council, for those agencies where the CIO has broad authority to manage all IT investments, great progress has been made to streamline and modernize the federal agency's footprint. For the others, where agency CIOs are only able to control pieces of the total IT footprint, it has been harder to achieve improvements.[22]

Current Administration Has Undertaken Efforts to Improve Federal IT

The current administration has initiated additional efforts aimed at improving federal IT, including digital services. Specifically, in March 2017, the administration established the Office of American Innovation, which has a mission to, among other things, make recommendations to the President on policies and plans aimed at improving federal government operations and services and on modernizing federal IT. In doing so, the office is to consult with both OMB and the Office of Science and Technology Policy on policies and plans intended to improve government operations and services, improve the quality of life for Americans, and spur job creation.[23]

In May 2017, the administration also established the American Technology Council, which has a goal of helping to transform and modernize federal agency IT and how the federal government uses and delivers digital services. The President is the chairman of this council, and the Federal CIO and the United States Digital Service[24] administrator are members.

---

[22]CIO Council, *State of Federal Information Technology* (Washington, D.C.: January 2017).

[23]The White House Office of Science and Technology Policy provides the President and others within the Executive Office of the President with advice on the scientific, engineering, and technological aspects of the economy, national security, homeland security, health, foreign relations, the environment, and the technological recovery and use of resources, among other topics.

[24]The United States Digital Service is an office within OMB which aims to improve the most important public-facing federal digital services.

Congress Has Taken Action to Continue Selected FITARA Provisions and Modernize Federal IT

Congress has recognized the importance of agencies' continued implementation of FITARA provisions, and has taken legislative action to extend selected provisions beyond their original dates of expiration. For example, Congress has passed legislation to:[25]

- remove the expiration date for enhanced transparency and improved risk management provisions, which were set to expire in 2019;

- remove the expiration date for portfolio review, which was set to expire in 2019; and

- extend the expiration date for FDCCI from 2018 to 2020.

In addition, Congress is considering legislation to ensure the availability of funding to help further agencies' efforts to modernize IT.[26] Specifically, recently proposed legislation calls for agencies to establish working capital funds for use in transitioning from legacy systems, as well as for addressing evolving threats to information security. The legislation also proposes the creation of a technology modernization fund within the Department of the Treasury, from which agencies could borrow money to retire and replace legacy systems as well as acquire or develop systems.

Agencies Have Taken Steps to Implement FITARA, but Additional Actions are Needed to Address Related Recommendations

Agencies have taken steps to improve the management of IT acquisitions and operations by implementing key FITARA initiatives. However, agencies would be better positioned to fully implement the law and, thus, realize billions in cost savings and additional management improvements, if they addressed the numerous recommendations we have made aimed at improving data center consolidation, increasing transparency via OMB's IT Dashboard, implementing incremental development, and managing software licenses.

---

[25]FITARA Enhancement Act of 2017, H.R. 3243, 115th Cong. (2017).

[26]National Defense Authorization Act for Fiscal Year 2018, H.R. 2810, 115th Cong., div. A, Title X, Subtitle H (as passed by the Senate on Sept. 18, 2017). A conference agreement on this legislation is pending.

Agencies Have Made Progress in Consolidating Data Centers, but Need to Take Action to Achieve Planned Cost Savings

One of the key initiatives to implement FITARA is data center consolidation. OMB established FDCCI in February 2010 to improve the efficiency, performance, and environmental footprint of federal data center activities, and the enactment of FITARA reinforced the initiative. However, in a series of reports that we issued from July 2011 through August 2017, we noted that, while data center consolidation could potentially save the federal government billions of dollars, weaknesses existed in several areas, including agencies' data center consolidation plans, data center optimization, and OMB's tracking and reporting on related cost savings.[27] In these reports, we made a matter for Congressional consideration, and a total of 160 recommendations to OMB and 24 agencies to improve the execution and oversight of the initiative. Most agencies and OMB agreed with our recommendations or had no comments. As of November 2017, 84 of these recommendations remained open.

For example, in May 2017, we reported[28] that the 24 agencies[29] participating in FDCCI collectively had made progress on their data center closure efforts. Specifically, as of August 2016, these agencies had identified a total of 9,995 data centers, of which they reported having closed 4,388, and having plans to close a total of 5,597 data centers

---

[27]GAO, *Data Center Optimization: Agencies Need to Address Challenges and Improve Progress to Achieve Cost Savings Goal*, GAO-17-448 (Washington, D.C.: Aug. 15, 2017); *Data Center Optimization: Agencies Need to Complete Plans to Address Inconsistencies in Reported Savings*, GAO-17-388 (Washington, D.C.: May 18, 2017); *Data Center Consolidation: Agencies Making Progress, but Planned Savings Goals Need to Be Established [Reissued on March 4, 2016]*, GAO-16-323 (Washington, D.C.: Mar. 3, 2016); *Data Center Consolidation: Reporting Can Be Improved to Reflect Substantial Planned Savings*, GAO-14-713 (Washington, D.C.: Sept. 25, 2014); *Data Center Consolidation: Strengthened Oversight Needed to Achieve Cost Savings Goal*, GAO-13-378 (Washington, D.C.: Apr. 23, 2013); *Data Center Consolidation: Agencies Making Progress on Efforts, but Inventories and Plans Need to Be Completed*, GAO-12-742 (Washington, D.C.: July 19, 2012); and *Data Center Consolidation: Agencies Need to Complete Inventories and Plans to Achieve Expected Savings*, GAO-11-565 (Washington, D.C.: July 19, 2011).

[28]GAO-17-388.

[29]The 24 agencies that FITARA requires to participate in FDCCI are the Departments of Agriculture, Commerce, Defense, Education, Energy, Health and Human Services, Homeland Security, Housing and Urban Development, the Interior, Justice, Labor, State, Transportation, the Treasury, and Veterans Affairs; the Environmental Protection Agency; General Services Administration; National Aeronautics and Space Administration; National Science Foundation; Nuclear Regulatory Commission; Office of Personnel Management; Small Business Administration; Social Security Administration; and U.S. Agency for International Development.

through fiscal year 2019. Notably, the Departments of Agriculture, Defense, the Interior, and the Treasury accounted for 84 percent of the completed closures.

In addition, that report noted that 18 of the 24 agencies had reported achieving about $2.3 billion collectively in cost savings and avoidances from their data center consolidation and optimization efforts from fiscal year 2012 through August 2016. The Departments of Commerce, Defense, Homeland Security, and the Treasury accounted for approximately $2.0 billion (or 87 percent) of the total.

Further, 23 agencies reported about $656 million collectively in planned savings for fiscal years 2016 through 2018. This is about $3.3 billion less than the estimated $4.0 billion in planned savings for fiscal years 2016 through 2018 that agencies reported to us in November 2015. Figure 3 presents a comparison of the amounts of cost savings and avoidances reported by agencies to OMB and the amounts the agencies reported to us.

Figure 3: Comparison of Fiscal Years 2016-2018 Planned Cost Savings and Avoidances Reported to GAO in November 2015 versus Those Reported to the Office of Management and Budget in April 2017

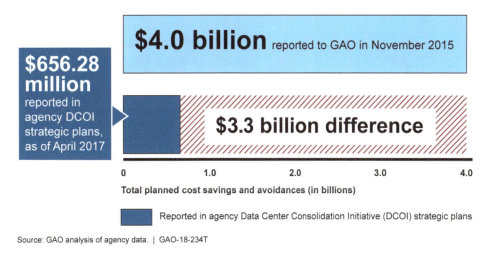

Source: GAO analysis of agency data. | GAO-18-234T

As mentioned previously, FITARA required agencies to submit multi-year strategies to achieve the consolidation and optimization of their data centers no later than the end of fiscal year 2016. Among other things, this strategy was to include such information as data center consolidation and optimization metrics, and year-by-year calculations of investments and cost savings through October 1, 2018.

Further, OMB's August 2016 guidance on data center optimization contained additional information for how agencies are to implement the strategic plan requirements of FITARA, and stated that agencies were required to publicly post their strategic plans to their agency-owned digital strategy websites by September 30, 2016.[30]

As of April 2017, only 7 of the 23 agencies that submitted their strategic plans—the Departments of Agriculture, Education, Homeland Security, and Housing and Urban Development; the General Services Administration; the National Science Foundation; and the Office of Personnel Management—had addressed all five elements required by the OMB memorandum implementing FITARA. The remaining 16 agencies either partially met or did not meet the requirements. For example, most agencies partially met or did not meet the requirements to provide information related to data center closures and cost savings metrics. The Department of Defense did not submit a plan and was rated as not meeting any of the requirements.

To better ensure that federal data center consolidation and optimization efforts improve governmental efficiency and achieve cost savings, in our May 2017 report, we recommended that 11 of the 24 agencies take action to ensure that the amounts of achieved data center cost savings and avoidances are consistent across all reporting mechanisms. We also recommended that 17 of the 24 agencies each take action to complete missing elements in their strategic plans and submit their plans to OMB in order to optimize their data centers and achieve cost savings. Twelve agencies agreed with our recommendations, 2 did not agree, and 10 agencies and OMB did not state whether they agreed or disagreed.

More recently, in August 2017, we reported that agencies needed to address challenges in optimizing their data centers in order to achieve cost savings.[31] Specifically, we noted that, according to the 24 agencies' data center consolidation initiative strategic plans as of April 2017, most agencies were not planning to meet OMB's optimization targets by the

---

[30]OMB, *Data Center Optimization Initiative (DCOI)*, Memorandum M-16-19 (Washington, D.C.: Aug. 1, 2016).

[31]GAO-17-448.

end of fiscal year 2018. Further, of the 24 agencies, 5—the Department of Commerce and the Environmental Protection Agency, National Science Foundation, Small Business Administration, and U.S. Agency for International Development—reported plans to fully meet their applicable targets by the end of fiscal year 2018;[32] 13 reported plans to meet some, but not all, of the targets; 4 reported that they did not plan to meet any targets; and 2 did not have a basis to report planned optimization milestones because they do not report having any agency-owned data centers. Figure 4 summarizes agencies' progress in meeting OMB's optimization targets as of February 2017, and planned progress to be achieved by September 2017 and September 2018, as of April 2017. Figure 4: Agency-Reported Plans to Meet or Exceed the Office of Management and Budget's (OMB) Data Center Optimization Targets

---

[32]U.S. Agency for International Development did not have any tiered data centers in its data center inventory. Therefore, the agency only had a basis to report on its plans to meet the one OMB optimization metric applicable to its non-tiered data centers (i.e., server utilization and automated monitoring).

Figure 4: Agency-Reported Plans to Meet or Exceed the Office of Management and Budget's (OMB) Data Center Optimization Targets

The following table represents the figure. Each value indicates the number of shaded boxes (out of 5 optimization targets) for each column.

Agency	Current progress from OMB's Information Technology Dashboard (as of February 2017)	Planned optimization performance from agency data center optimization strategic plan (as of April 2017)	
		September 2017	September 2018
Department of Agriculture	1	1	1
Department of Commerce	0	3	5
Department of Defense	0	0	0
Department of Education[a]	Not applicable	Not applicable	Not applicable
Department of Energy	0	0	4
Department of Health and Human Services	1	1	1
Department of Homeland Security	0	0	0
Department of Housing and Urban Development[a]	Not applicable	Not applicable	Not applicable
Department of the Interior	0	0	0
Department of Justice	0	0	1
Department of Labor	0	0	4
Department of State	1	2	2
Department of Transportation	0	0	0
Department of the Treasury	0	1	2
Department of Veterans Affairs	1	0	3
Environmental Protection Agency	3	2	5
General Services Administration	1	1	1
National Aeronautics and Space Administration	0	0	1
National Science Foundation[b]	0	3	5
Nuclear Regulatory Commission	1	1	1
Office of Personnel Management	1	1	4
Small Business Administration	0	1	5
Social Security Administration	3	3	3
U.S. Agency for International Development[c]	0	0	1

Source: GAO analysis of OMB Information Technology Dashboard and agency data. | GAO-18-234T

Note: The five boxes in each column represent OMB's five optimization targets relative to (1) server utilization and automated monitoring; (2) energy metering; (3) power usage effectiveness; (4) facility utilization; and (5) virtualization. The shaded areas identify agencies' current and planned progress in meeting or exceeding OMB's fiscal year 2018 target for each metric.

[a] Agency did not have any reported agency-owned data centers in its inventory and, therefore, did not have a basis to measure and report on optimization progress.

FITARA required OMB to establish a data center optimization metric specific to measuring server efficiency, and required agencies to report on progress in meeting this metric. To effectively measure progress against this metric, OMB directed agencies to replace the manual collection and reporting of systems, software, and hardware inventory housed within agency-owned data centers with automated monitoring tools and to complete this effort no later than the end of fiscal year 2018. Agencies were required to report progress in implementing automated monitoring tools and server utilization averages at each data center as part of their quarterly data center inventory reporting to OMB.

As of February 2017, 4 of the 22 agencies reporting agency-owned data centers in their inventory[33]— the National Aeronautics and Space Administration, National Science Foundation, Social Security Administration, and U.S. Agency for International Development—reported that they had implemented automated monitoring tools at all of their data centers. Further, 10 reported that they had implemented automated monitoring tools at between 1 and 57 percent of their centers, and 8 had not yet begun to report the implementation of these tools. In total, the 22 agencies reported that automated tools were implemented at 123 (or about 3 percent) of the 4,528 total agency-owned data centers, while the remaining 4,405 (or about 97 percent) of these data centers were not reported as having these tools implemented. Figure 5 summarizes the number of agency-reported data centers with automated monitoring tools implemented, including the number of tiered and non-tiered centers.

---

[33]Two agencies—the Department of Education and Housing and Urban Development—do not have any agency-owned data centers; therefore, they do not have a basis for implementing automated monitoring tools.

Figure 5: Number of Agency-Reported Data Centers with Automated Monitoring Tools Implemented, as of February 2017

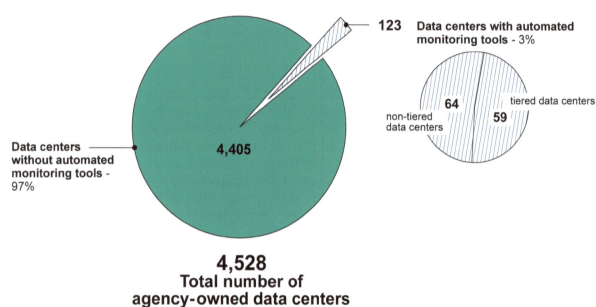

123 **Data centers with automated monitoring tools** - 3%

non-tiered data centers 64   59 tiered data centers

Data centers without automated monitoring tools - 97%

4,405

4,528
Total number of
agency-owned data centers

Source: GAO analysis of Office of Management and Budget and agency data. | GAO-18-234T

To address challenges in optimizing federal data centers, in our August 2017 report, we made recommendations to 18 agencies and OMB. Ten agencies agreed with our recommendations, three agencies partially agreed, and six (including OMB) did not state whether they agreed or disagreed.

Risks Need to Be Fully Considered When Agencies Rate Their Major Investments on OMB's IT Dashboard

To facilitate transparency across the government in acquiring and managing IT investments, OMB established a public website—the IT Dashboard—to provide detailed information on major investments at 26 agencies, including ratings of their performance against cost and schedule targets. Among other things, agencies are to submit ratings from their CIOs, which, according to OMB's instructions, should reflect the level of risk facing an investment relative to that investment's ability to accomplish its goals. In this regard, FITARA includes a requirement for CIOs to categorize their major IT investment risks in accordance with OMB guidance.[34]

---

[34]40 U.S.C. § 11302(c)(3)(C).

Over the past 6 years, we have issued a series of reports about the Dashboard that noted both significant steps OMB has taken to enhance the oversight, transparency, and accountability of federal IT investments by creating its Dashboard, as well as concerns about the accuracy and reliability of the data.[35] In total, we have made 47 recommendations to OMB and federal agencies to help improve the accuracy and reliability of the information on the Dashboard and to increase its availability. Most agencies agreed with our recommendations or had no comments. As of November 2017, 25 recommendations remained open.

In June 2016, we determined that 13 of the 15 agencies selected for in-depth review had not fully considered risks when rating their major investments on the Dashboard. Specifically, our assessments of risk for 95 investments at the 15 selected agencies[36] matched the CIO ratings posted on the Dashboard 22 times, showed more risk 60 times, and showed less risk 13 times. Figure 6 summarizes how our assessments compared to the selected investments' CIO ratings.

---

[35]GAO, *IT Dashboard: Agencies Need to Fully Consider Risks When Rating Their Major Investments,* GAO-16-494 (Washington, D.C.: June 2, 2016); *IT Dashboard: Agencies Are Managing Investment Risk, but Related Ratings Need to Be More Accurate and Available,* GAO-14-64 (Washington, D.C.: Dec. 12, 2013); *IT Dashboard: Opportunities Exist to Improve Transparency and Oversight of Investment Risk at Select Agencies,* GAO-13-98 (Washington, D.C.: Oct. 16, 2012); *IT Dashboard: Accuracy Has Improved, and Additional Efforts Are under Way to Better Inform Decision Making,* GAO-12-210 (Washington, D.C.: Nov. 7, 2011); *Information Technology: OMB Has Made Improvements to Its Dashboard, but Further Work Is Needed by Agencies and OMB to Ensure Data Accuracy,* GAO-11-262 (Washington, D.C.: Mar. 15, 2011); and *Information Technology: OMB's Dashboard Has Increased Transparency and Oversight, but Improvements Needed,* GAO-10-701 (Washington, D.C.: July 16, 2010).

[36]The 15 selected agencies were the Departments of Agriculture, Commerce, Defense, Education, Energy, Health and Human Services, Homeland Security, the Interior, State, Transportation, the Treasury, and Veterans Affairs; the Environmental Protection Agency; General Services Administration; and Social Security Administration.

Figure 6: Comparison of Selected Investments' April 2015 Chief Information Officer Ratings to GAO's Assessments

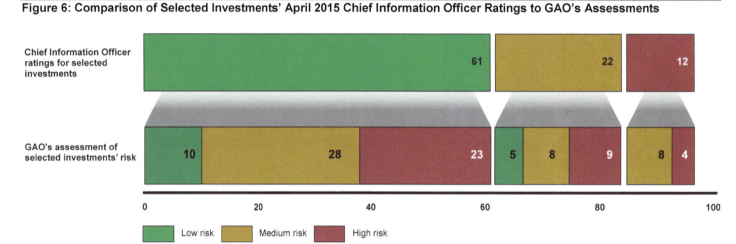

Source: GAO's assessment of data from the Office of Management and Budget's Information Technology Dashboard. | GAO-18-234T

Aside from the inherently judgmental nature of risk ratings, we identified three factors which contributed to differences between our assessments and the CIO ratings:

- Forty of the 95 CIO ratings were not updated during April 2015 (the month we conducted our review), which led to differences between our assessments and the CIOs' ratings. This underscores the importance of frequent rating updates, which help to ensure that the information on the Dashboard is timely and accurately reflects recent changes to investment status.

- Three agencies' rating processes spanned longer than 1 month. Longer processes mean that CIO ratings are based on older data, and may not reflect the current level of investment risk.

- Seven agencies' rating processes did not focus on active risks. According to OMB's guidance, CIO ratings should reflect the CIO's assessment of the risk and the investment's ability to accomplish its goals. CIO ratings that do no incorporate active risks increase the chance that ratings overstate the likelihood of investment success.

As a result, we concluded that the associated risk rating processes used by the 15 agencies were generally understating the level of an investment's risk, raising the likelihood that critical federal investments in IT are not receiving the appropriate levels of oversight.

To better ensure that the Dashboard ratings more accurately reflect risk, we made 25 recommendations to 15 agencies to improve the quality and frequency of their CIO ratings. Twelve agencies generally agreed with or did not comment on the recommendations and three agencies disagreed, stating that their CIO ratings were adequate. However, we noted that weaknesses in these three agencies' processes still existed and that we continued to believe our recommendations were appropriate.

Agencies Need to Increase Their Use of Incremental Development Practices

OMB has emphasized the need to deliver investments in smaller parts, or increments, in order to reduce risk, deliver capabilities more quickly, and facilitate the adoption of emerging technologies. In 2010, it called for agencies' major investments to deliver functionality every 12 months and, since 2012, every 6 months. Subsequently, FITARA codified a requirement that agency CIOs certify that IT investments are adequately implementing incremental development, as defined in the capital planning guidance issued by OMB.[37] Further, subsequent OMB guidance on the law's implementation, issued in June 2015, directed agency CIOs to define processes and policies for their agencies which ensure that they certify that IT resources are adequately implementing incremental development.[38]

However, in May 2014, we reported[39] that 66 of 89 selected investments at five major agencies[40] did not plan to deliver capabilities in 6-month cycles, and less than half of these investments planned to deliver functionality in 12-month cycles. We also reported that only one of the five agencies had complete incremental development policies. Accordingly, we recommended that OMB clarify its guidance on incremental development and that the selected agencies update their associated policies to comply with OMB's revised guidance (once made available), and consider the factors identified in our report when doing so.

Four of the six agencies agreed with our recommendations or had no comments, one agency partially agreed, and the remaining agency

---

[37]40 U.S.C. § 11319(b)(1)(B)(ii).

[38]OMB, Memorandum M-15-14.

[39]GAO, *Information Technology: Agencies Need to Establish and Implement Incremental Development Policies*, GAO-14-361 (Washington, D.C.: May 1, 2014).

[40]These five agencies are the Departments of Defense, Health and Human Services, Homeland Security, Transportation, and Veterans Affairs.

disagreed with the recommendations. The agency that disagreed did not believe that its recommendations should be dependent upon OMB taking action to update guidance. In response, we noted that only one of the recommendations to that agency depended upon OMB action, and we maintained that the action was warranted and could be implemented.

Subsequently, in August 2016, we reported[41] that agencies had not fully implemented incremental development practices for their software development projects. Specifically, we noted that, as of August 31, 2015, 22 federal agencies[42] had reported on the Dashboard that 300 of 469 active software development projects (approximately 64 percent) were planning to deliver usable functionality every 6 months for fiscal year 2016, as required by OMB guidance. The remaining 169 projects (or 36 percent) that were reported as not planning to deliver functionality every 6 months, agencies provided a variety of explanations for not achieving that goal. These included project complexity, the lack of an established project release schedule, or that the project was not a software development project.

Further, in conducting an in-depth review of seven selected agencies' software development projects,[43] we determined that 45 percent of the projects delivered functionality every 6 months for fiscal year 2015 and 55 percent planned to do so in fiscal year 2016. However, significant differences existed between the delivery rates that the agencies reported to us and what they reported on the Dashboard. For example, for four agencies (the Departments of Commerce, Education, Health and Human Services, and Treasury), the percentage of delivery reported to us was at least 10 percentage points lower than what was reported on the Dashboard. These differences were due to (1) our identification of fewer

---

[41]GAO, *Information Technology Reform: Agencies Need to Increase Their Use of Incremental Development Practices,* GAO-16-469 (Washington, D.C.: Aug. 16, 2016).

[42]These 22 agencies are the Departments of Agriculture, Commerce, Defense, Education, Energy, Health and Human Services, Homeland Security, Housing and Urban Development, the Interior, Justice, Labor, State, Transportation, the Treasury, and Veterans Affairs; the Environmental Protection Agency, General Services Administration, National Archives and Records Administration, Office of Personnel Management, Small Business Administration, Social Security Administration, and U.S. Agency for International Development.

[43]These seven agencies are the Departments of Commerce, Defense, Education, Health and Human Services, Homeland Security, Transportation, and the Treasury. These agencies were chosen because they reported a minimum of 12 investments that were at least 50 percent or more in development on the Dashboard for fiscal year 2015.

software development projects than agencies reported on the Dashboard and (2) the fact that information reported to us was generally more current than the information reported on the Dashboard.

We concluded that, by not having up-to-date information on the Dashboard about whether the project is a software development project and about the extent to which projects are delivering functionality, these seven agencies were at risk that OMB and key stakeholders may make decisions regarding the agencies' investments without the most current and accurate information. As such, we recommended that the seven selected agencies review major IT investment project data reported on the Dashboard and update the information as appropriate, ensuring that these data are consistent across all reporting channels.

Finally, while OMB has issued guidance requiring agency CIOs to certify that each major IT investment's plan for the current year adequately implements incremental development, only three agencies (the Departments of Commerce, Homeland Security, and Transportation) had defined processes and policies intended to ensure that the CIOs certify that major IT investments are adequately implementing incremental development.[44] Accordingly, we recommended that the remaining four agencies—the Departments of Defense, Education, Health and Human Services, and the Treasury—establish policies and processes for certifying that major IT investments adequately use incremental development.

The Departments of Education and Health and Human Services agreed with our recommendation, while the Department of Defense disagreed and stated that its existing policies address the use of incremental development. However, we noted that the department's policies did not comply with OMB's guidance and that we continued to believe our recommendation was appropriate. The Department of the Treasury did not comment on its recommendation.

More recently, in November 2017, we reported that agencies needed to improve their certification of incremental development.[45] Specifically, agencies reported that 62 percent of major IT software development investments were certified by the agency CIO for implementing adequate

---

[44]Office of Management and Budget, *FY2017 IT Budget – Capital Planning Guidance.*

[45]GAO, *Information Technology Reform: Agencies Need to Improve Certification of Incremental Development,* GAO-18-148 (Washington, D.C.: Nov. 7, 2017).

incremental development in fiscal year 2017, as required by FITARA as of August 2016. Table 1 identifies the number of federal agency major IT software development investments certified for adequate incremental development, as reported on the IT Dashboard for fiscal year 2017.

Table 1: Federal Agency Major Information Technology (IT) Software Development Investments Certified for Adequate Incremental Development, as Reported on the IT Dashboard for Fiscal Year 2017

Agency	Number of major investments	Number of investments certified for adequate incremental development	Percent of investments certified for adequate incremental development
U.S. Department of Agriculture	7	4	57%
Department of Commerce	11	10	91%
Department of Defense	33	10	30%
Department of Education	7	6	86%
Department of Energy	3	1	33%
Department of Health and Human Services	24	20	83%
Department of Homeland Security	10	6	60%
Department of Housing and Urban Development	1	1	100%
Department of the Interior	6	4	67%
Department of Justice	2	2	100%
Department of Labor	1	1	100%
Department of State	5	5	100%
Department of Transportation	12	3	25%
Department of the Treasury	10	3	30%
Department of Veterans Affairs	10	10	100%
Environmental Protection Agency	1	1	100%
General Services Administration	7	7	100%
Office of Personnel Management	3	3	100%
Small Business Administration	2	2	100%
Social Security Administration	10	3	30%
U.S. Agency for International Development	1	1	100%
Total	**166**	**103**	**62%**

Source: GAO analysis of IT Dashboard data as of August 31, 2016. | GAO-18-234T

Officials from 21 of the 24 agencies in our review reported that challenges hindered their ability to implement incremental development, which included: (1) inefficient governance processes; (2) procurement delays; and (3) organizational changes associated with transitioning from a traditional software methodology that takes years to deliver a product, to incremental development, which delivers products in shorter time frames. Nevertheless, 21 agencies reported that the certification process was beneficial because they used the information from the process to assist with identifying investments that could more effectively use an incremental approach, and used lessons learned to improve the agencies' incremental processes.

In addition, as of August 2017, only 4 of the 24 agencies had clearly defined CIO incremental development certification policies and processes that contained descriptions of the role of the CIO in the process and how the CIO's certification will be documented; and included definitions of incremental development and time frames for delivering functionality consistent with OMB guidance. Figure 7 summarizes our analysis of agencies' policies for CIO certification of the adequate use of incremental development in IT investments.

Figure 7: Analysis of Agencies' Policies for Chief Information Officer Certification of the Adequate Use of Incremental Development in Information Technology Investments

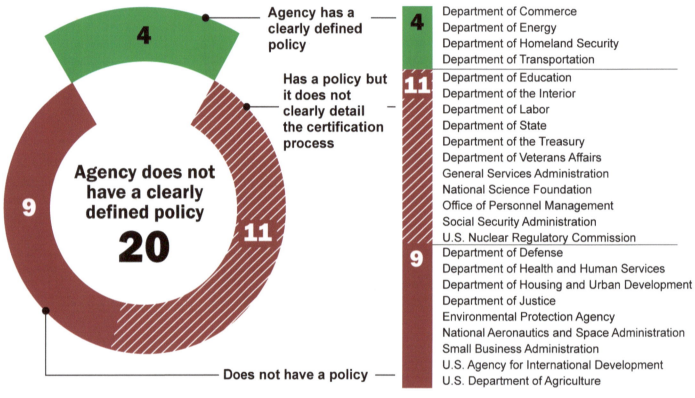

Source: GAO analysis of agency Chief Information Officer certification policies and processes. | GAO-18-234T

Lastly, we reported that OMB's capital planning guidance for fiscal year 2018[46] (issued in June 2016) lacked clarity regarding how agencies were to address the requirement for certifying adequate incremental development. While the 2018 guidance stated that agency CIOs are to provide the certifications needed to demonstrate compliance with FITARA, the guidance did not include a specific reference to the provision requiring CIO certification of adequate incremental development. We noted that, as a result of this change, OMB placed the burden on agencies to know and understand how to demonstrate compliance with FITARA's incremental development provision. Further, because of the lack of clarity in the guidance as to what agencies were to provide, OMB

---

[46]OMB, FY 2017 IT Budget–Capital Planning Guidance.

could not demonstrate how the fiscal year 2018 guidance ensured that agencies provided the certifications specifically called for in the law.

Accordingly, in August 2017, OMB issued its fiscal year 2019 guidance,[47] which addressed the weaknesses we identified in the previous fiscal year's guidance. Specifically, the revised guidance requires agency CIOs to make an explicit statement regarding the extent to which the CIO is able to certify the use of incremental development, and to include a copy of that statement in the agency's public congressional budget justification materials. As part of the statement, an agency CIO must also identify which specific bureaus or offices are using incremental development on all of their investments.

In our November 2017 report, we made 19 recommendations to 17 agencies to improve reporting and certification of incremental development. Eleven agencies agreed with our recommendations, 1 partially agreed, and 5 did not state whether they agreed or disagreed. OMB disagreed with several of our conclusions, which we continued to believe were valid.

In total, from May 2014 through November 2017, we have made 42 recommendations to OMB and agencies to improve their implementation of incremental development. As of November 2017, 34 of our recommendations remained open.

Agencies Need to Better Manage Software Licenses to Achieve Savings

Federal agencies engage in thousands of software licensing agreements annually. The objective of software license management is to manage, control, and protect an organization's software assets. Effective management of these licenses can help avoid purchasing too many licenses, which can result in unused software, as well as too few licenses, which can result in noncompliance with license terms and cause the imposition of additional fees.

As part of its PortfolioStat initiative, OMB has developed policy that addresses software licenses. This policy requires agencies to conduct an annual, agency-wide IT portfolio review to, among other things, reduce commodity IT spending. Such areas of spending could include software licenses.

---

[47]OMB, FY 2019 IT Budget–Capital Planning Guidance.

In May 2014, we reported on federal agencies' management of software licenses and determined that better management was needed to achieve significant savings government-wide.[48] In particular, 22 of the 24 major agencies did not have comprehensive license policies and only 2 had comprehensive license inventories. In addition, we identified five leading software license management practices, and the agencies' implementation of these practices varied.

As a result of agencies' mixed management of software licensing, agencies' oversight of software license spending was limited or lacking, thus potentially leading to missed savings. However, the potential savings could be significant considering that, in fiscal year 2012, 1 major federal agency reported saving approximately $181 million by consolidating its enterprise license agreements, even when its oversight process was ad hoc. Accordingly, we recommended that OMB issue needed guidance to agencies; we also made 135 recommendations to the 24 agencies to improve their policies and practices for managing licenses. Among other things, we recommended that the agencies regularly track and maintain a comprehensive inventory of software licenses and analyze the inventory to identify opportunities to reduce costs and better inform investment decision making.

Most agencies generally agreed with the recommendations or had no comments. As of November 2017, 112 of the recommendations had not been implemented. Table 2 reflects the extent to which agencies implemented recommendations in these areas.

---

[48]GAO, *Federal Software Licenses: Better Management Needed to Achieve Significant Savings Government-Wide,* GAO-14-413 (Washington, D.C.: May 22, 2014).

Table 2: Agencies' Implementation of Software License Management Recommendations

Agency	Tracks and maintains a comprehensive inventory	Uses inventory to make decisions and reduce costs
Department of Agriculture	●	●
Department of Commerce	◑	●
Department of Defense	◑	◑
Department of Education	●	●
Department of Energy	◑	◑
Department of Health and Human Services	◑	◑
Department of Homeland Security	◑	◑
Department of Housing and Urban Development	◑	◑
Department of Justice	◑	◑
Department of Labor	●	◑
Department of State	◑	◑
Department of the Interior	◑	◑
Department of the Treasury	◑	◑
Department of Transportation	◑	◑
Department of Veterans Affairs	●	●
Environmental Protection Agency	◑	◑
General Services Administration	●	●
National Aeronautics and Space Administration	●	●
Nuclear Regulatory Commission	◑	◑
National Science Foundation	◑	◑
Office of Personnel Management	◑	◑
Small Business Administration	◑	◑
Social Security Administration	◑	◑
U.S. Agency for International Development	●	●

Key:

● Fully—the agency provided evidence that it fully addressed this recommendation

◑ Partially—the agency had plans to address this recommendation

Source: GAO analysis. | GAO-18-234T

In conclusion, with the enactment of FITARA, the federal government has an opportunity to save billions of dollars; improve the transparency and management of IT acquisitions and operations; and to strengthen the authority of CIOs to provide needed direction and oversight. The forum we held also recommended that CIOs be given more authority, and noted the important role played by the Federal CIO.

Most agencies have taken steps to improve the management of IT acquisitions and operations by implementing key FITARA initiatives, including data center consolidation, efforts to increase transparency via OMB's IT Dashboard, incremental development, and management of software licenses; and they have continued to address recommendations we have made over the past several years. However, additional improvements are needed, and further efforts by OMB and federal agencies to implement our previous recommendations would better position them to fully implement FITARA.

To help ensure that these efforts succeed, OMB's and agencies' continued implementation of FITARA is essential. In addition, we will continue to monitor agencies' implementation of our previous recommendations.

Chairmen Meadows and Hurd, Ranking Members Connolly and Kelly, and Members of the Subcommittees, this completes my prepared statement. I would be pleased to respond to any questions that you may have at this time.

GAO Contacts and Staff Acknowledgments

If you or your staff have any questions about this testimony, please contact Dave Powner, Director, Information Technology at (202) 512-9286 or pownerd@gao.gov. Contact points for our Offices of Congressional Relations and Public Affairs may be found on the last page of this statement. GAO staff who made key contributions to this testimony are Kevin Walsh (Assistant Director), Chris Businsky, Rebecca Eyler, Meredith Raymond, and Bradley Roach (Analyst in Charge).

www.ingramcontent.com/pod-product-compliance
Lightning Source LLC
Chambersburg PA
CBHW041430050326
40690CB00002B/490